Penguin
LIVES

Julia Child

A LIPPER™/VIKING BOOK

PUBLISHED TITLES IN THE PENGUIN LIVES SERIES:

Larry McMurtry on Crazy Horse

Edmund White on Marcel Proust · Peter Gay on Mozart

Garry Wills on Saint Augustine · Jonathan Spence on Mao Zedong

Edna O'Brien on James Joyce · Douglas Brinkley on Rosa Parks

Elizabeth Hardwick on Herman Melville

Louis Auchincloss on Woodrow Wilson

Mary Gordon on Joan of Arc

Sherwin B. Nuland on Leonardo da Vinci

Nigel Nicolson on Virginia Woolf · Carol Shields on Jane Austen

Karen Armstrong on the Buddha · R. W. B. Lewis on Dante

Francine du Plessix Gray on Simone Weil

Patricia Bosworth on Marlon Brando

Wayne Koestenbaum on Andy Warhol

Thomas Cahill on Pope John XXIII

Marshall Frady on Martin Luther King, Jr.

Paul Johnson on Napoleon · Jane Smiley on Charles Dickens

John Keegan on Winston Churchill

Robert V. Remini on Joseph Smith

Thomas Keneally on Abraham Lincoln

Bobbie Ann Mason on Elvis Presley

Roy Blount, Jr., on Robert E. Lee

Kathryn Harrison on Saint Thérèse of Lisieux

Martin Marty on Martin Luther

Tom Wicker on George Herbert Walker Bush

Ada Louise Huxtable on Frank Lloyd Wright

FORTHCOMING:

Jimmy Breslin on Branch Rickey

LAURA SHAPIRO

Julia Child

A Penguin Life

A LIPPER™/VIKING BOOK

VIKING
Published by the Penguin Group
Penguin Group (USA) Inc., 375 Hudson Street,
New York, New York 10014, U.S.A.
Penguin Group (Canada), 90 Eglinton Avenue East, Suite 700, Toronto, Ontario, Canada M4P 2Y3 (a division of Pearson Penguin Canada Inc.) · Penguin Books Ltd, 80 Strand, London WC2R 0RL, England · Penguin Ireland, 25 St. Stephen's Green, Dublin 2, Ireland (a division of Penguin Books Ltd) · Penguin Books Australia Ltd, 250 Camberwell Road, Camberwell, Victoria 3124, Australia (a division of Pearson Australia Group Pty Ltd) · Penguin Books India Pvt Ltd, 11 Community Centre, Panchsheel Park, New Delhi–110 017, India · Penguin Group (NZ), 67 Apollo Drive, Mairangi Bay, Auckland 1311, New Zealand (a division of Pearson New Zealand Ltd) · Penguin Books (South Africa) (Pty) Ltd, 24 Sturdee Avenue, Rosebank, Johannesburg 2196, South Africa

Penguin Books Ltd, Registered Offices: 80 Strand, London WC2R 0RL, England

First published in 2007 by Viking Penguin, a member of Penguin Group (USA) Inc.

1 3 5 7 9 10 8 6 4 2

A portion of this book appeared in different form as "Sacred Cows and Dreamberries: In Search of the Flavor of France," *Gastronomica* 5, no. 3 (Summer 2005).

Page 186 constitutes an extension of this copyright page.

LIBRARY OF CONGRESS CATALOGING-IN-PUBLICATION DATA
Shapiro, Laura.
Julia Child / Laura Shapiro.
p. cm.—(A Penguin life)
ISBN 978-0-670-03839-8
1. Child, Julia. 2. Cooks—United States—Biography. I. Title.
TX649.C47S53 2007
641.5092—dc22 2006052560

Printed in the United States of America
Set in Walbaum
Designed by Francesca Belanger

To Barbara Haber

PREFACE

IT'S A BIG, RAW GOOSE, naked as a baby, and she's holding it up by its massive wings, gleefully wiggling them before the camera as if she'd like to waltz around the kitchen with her magnificent bird. "A ten-pound beauty!" she exclaims. "You can cut it all up, simmer it in wine, serve it with a delicious sauce—see how to ragout a goose, today on *The French Chef*!"

Julia Child loved handling food. She loved slathering great gobs of butter around a pan with her bare hand and plunging a forefinger into a thick swirl of custard to see how warm it was getting as she stirred; sometimes, while she was showing off an array of ingredients, she couldn't help patting them affectionately. But nothing made her gleam with pleasure like the prospect of getting her hands into the fresh and glistening flesh of an animal—a rump of veal, a goose, a suckling pig, a giant monkfish. When she explained the different cuts of beef on her legendary public television series *The French Chef*, she used her own body as the butcher's chart, twisting to display her back or side as if to make clear the intimate relationship between the cook and the meat. "To Ragout a Goose" was first aired on *The French Chef* in November 1972, long past the time when preparations for dinner in America began with domestic butchering. Most of Julia's viewers encountered poultry only after it had been cleaned, cut into pieces, and wrapped in cellophane—thoroughly denatured, that is, and ready for recipes. Julia never quarreled with convenience measures that would encourage more people to get into the kitchen, but she thought everyone should be able to take apart an animal easily and correctly. She knew there were squeamish cooks out there, not to mention vegetarians, because she got anguished letters from them all the time; but it was difficult for her to believe that people willingly surrendered their appetites to such trepidations. The idea of a self-imposed barrier between the cook and the food—whether that barrier represented physical, mental, emotional, or moral reluctance—astonished and dismayed her. Besides, if you were going to cook goose, one of Julia's all-time favorite foods, you had to bring it home whole, since it wasn't available in America in any other form. And she very much wanted Americans to cook goose. She had planned this lesson in part because it gave her a chance to demonstrate some of the most important tools in her entire *batterie de cuisine:* good, sharp knives and the courage to begin.

"After your goose is all defrosted, the first thing you do is to take out the fat and the giblets," she explained to viewers, with the goose splayed out on the counter in front of her. Eagerly, she reached inside. "There's lots of fat which is all attached to the back end, or the vent as it's politely called," she noted, gathering chunks of fat and putting them aside. "You want to save all of this fat, because it's wonderful to render." Her voice, a warm and hearty foghorn, swooped through each sentence, landing briefly on this word or that as it caught her fancy. To her evident surprise, after groping for the neck and giblets, she came up empty-handed—"For some reason, it doesn't have any"—but she did retrieve the liver, which she displayed for comparison purposes next to a life-size photograph of a fresh foie gras. "The large lobe is about seven inches long, from there to there," she pointed out admiringly. "The geese in France, in the foie gras country, are raised just for their livers, and that's why you can often buy goose by the piece, which you can't here."

Then she picked up a huge cleaver and began to butcher. "Whang!" The end of a wing flew off. With a smaller knife she slit the goose down the backbone and removed a leg and the rest of the wing ("As you notice, I've taken off a little bit of the breast along with the wing to make a better serving"), but instead of finishing the job on that goose, she pulled a second goose out in front of the camera. This one was further along in the butchering process; hence she was able to hold up its raw, gaping body to show exactly how the leg and wing had been attached. Then she attacked the second goose with one bare hand and a knife, scraping vigorously through skin and fat and meat, feeling her way around the body as she sought the precise location of various joints. "Here's what you're looking for: it's that ball joint that attaches the wing to the shoulder," she reported as the camera focused on her fast-moving hands. "There's the small of your back there, so get that out first, and there's your knee—and lifting up the knee, slit the skin. And you're raising up the thigh and the leg at the same time." When she had the bird in pieces, she swiftly knifed away the fatty skin—"Look at all the fat there, that's about . . . heavens . . . almost half an inch of fat"—and then proudly displayed the results. "You have three and a half pounds of fat and fatty skin pieces, and you have about two and a quarter pounds of carcass and wing ends and scraps. You have really less than four pounds of meat, but you're paying for all of this so you might as well use it. Render the fat and turn the scraps into soup stock, because it makes a delicious soup."

The pile of goose parts on the counter looked remarkably fresh and tidy, considering what they had gone through. "Now you're ready to cook the goose," she announced, and deftly floured the pieces by hand, turning and daubing them until each was lightly coated. "I never like to shake things in a paper bag with flour. It seems too ladies' magaziney for me." While the pieces were browning in goose fat, she brought out other elements of the ragout in various stages of completion—the onions, the lardons, the cabbage—and concisely demonstrated the crucial steps in their preparation. When the goose was browned, it went into the pan with the onions and lardons, and Julia added the wine, the stock, and the herbs. Her bird was now all set for a long simmer in the oven. Smiling down at the pieces that were jutting out from their cozy, aromatic bath, she tucked a sheet of wax paper over them. "Particularly because the goose was peeled, I like to protect it," she said fondly.

As soon as the goose went into the oven, she turned to a second oven and triumphantly pulled out her "ready" goose—a ragout that had been fully prepared before the show. Arranging the tender, fragrant pieces of goose on a bed of noodles, spooning the cabbage alongside them, she became so absorbed she sometimes fell silent until she remembered she was supposed to be talking. Yet even her silence was energetic: the attention she was pouring into this luscious-looking ragout as she readied it for the dining room was as vigorous as the actual cooking had been. "I like to serve things all on the same plate if there's room, because I think it's more attractive, though it's often difficult to get a big enough platter," she mused aloud as she worked. "Last time we were over in France I got some down near Nice and sent them over." She reached for a dish of parsley. "And then if you feel it needs a little more decoration—a typical parsley garnish."

Seated in the dining room with the platter in front of her, she was glowing: this was the culmination of the whole ardent enterprise. She picked up a plate and showed how to serve the ragout, and as she did so—perhaps it was the lighting, perhaps it was a trick of the imagination—suddenly we were seated at the table with her. Before our own hungry eyes, the camera zeroed in on the plate while Julia filled it, and we listened to her avid description of what we were going to eat. "This person is going to get a lovely big drumstick, and a nice handful of noodles, and some of this beautiful fresh cabbage. And then a little bit of your sauce on top." We could taste every morsel as she lifted it, we could taste the wine—"your very best red Burgundy." During the last moments of the show, she was so absorbed in serving a second portion that she almost forgot to look up for her sign-off. "This is Julia Child. *Bon appétit!*"

Julia Child was unlike any other celebrity in America. People gawked at her in restaurants, of course; greeted her joyfully on the street; excitedly pointed her out to one another when they glimpsed her in an airport; and crowded into bookstores whenever she arrived to sign copies of her latest cookbook. None of this was out of the ordinary in the realms of fame. What was unique about Julia was the quality of the emotion she inspired, which was remarkably direct and pure. Julia attracted love, torrents of it, a steady outpouring of delighted love that began with the first pilot episode of *The French Chef* in 1962 and continued through and beyond her death in 2004. As a fan in California once wrote, "Whenever your name comes up, people smile." And whenever her name came up, it was Julia, just Julia. "I feel that I know you so well that I take the liberty to call you by your first name," wrote one of the thousands of people who after discovering *The French Chef* sat down to thank her. "I say Julia, as I have come to know you personally thru Television. . . ." "I call you by your first name since I feel I know you so well from your program. . . ." "Perhaps you do not mind that I refer to you fondly as 'Julia' because to me you are a very dear friend. . . ." Letters piled up at every public television station that aired her series—letters, handwritten and typewritten, from men and women, often from children, and sometimes in verse. Most often people asked for recipes; other times they reported on what they had successfully made for dinner, thanks to Julia; many wanted to find out what kind of electric mixer or blender she was using, or where they could buy a whisk and a copper bowl for beating egg whites. But again and again, they wrote about love. "We love every swipe of your sticky hands. . . ." "Our mouths water ever so often and our hearts laugh. . . ." "PLEASE CONTINUE AS YOU ARE!" "Let me start first by saying—we love you, we love you, we love you!" "We love you, Julia!" Every television star had a following, but Julia was the only professional on screen whose appeal sprang directly from her own personality, unmediated by scriptwriters or guests. She played no role, not even the role of cooking teacher; she portrayed no fictional character; no political or religious agenda drove her contagious passion; she never gazed into the camera to discuss war and politics and thereby acquire the gravitas that made newscasters appear important. What viewers loved was the Julia they saw on television and believed in wholeheartedly—"your natural manner," "your honesty"—and they were not mistaken.

Julia on television was Julia cooking; and to watch her cook was to see every dimension of herself fully engaged. She cooked with mind, body, and spirit—the way dancers dance and musicians play their instruments—though Julia's work on-screen was more like a dancer's rehearsal session than an actual performance of *Swan Lake*. The goal was not to create a flawless fantasy, but to summon the technique and wisdom that are the essential elements of the discipline. Cooking was fun for Julia, and she wanted everyone else to experience it that way, too, but fun didn't mean frivolity to her. It meant that you knew what you were doing, that you had absorbed the skills and understood the procedures and now took great pleasure in the demands of the work. From the beginning, Julia was determined to prepare food on television in such a way that viewers would take cooking seriously even if the show itself was lighthearted. The "ladies' magaziney" element in cooking—an approach that fussed endlessly over shortcuts without teaching anything useful about either cooking or eating—struck her as a Pied Piper, all too capable of enticing Americans to their culinary doom. A few months before the series made its debut, executives at WGBH-TV began tinkering with the proposed title, trying to come up with something that sounded breezier and less intimidating than *The French Chef.* How about, for instance, "Looking at Cooking"? Julia stood firm. *The French Chef*, she told them, was a title that said exactly what she wanted to say. "It is short, to the point, dignified, glamorous, and appeals to men as well as women. . . . Something like 'Looking at Cooking,' or variations, sounds cheesy, little-womanish, cute, amateurish." Not that she ever represented herself as being, literally, either French or a chef. On-screen and off-, she was an American home cook, and a proud one. But she was also an expert with years of study and experience behind every recipe she prepared, and she had no intention of allowing herself or her chosen work to appear trivial.

The WGBH executives were wrong: nobody was intimidated by *The French Chef*, though there were certainly viewers who were quite content to stay right there in the living room and let Julia do the cooking. Even her friends, most of whom were very good cooks themselves, drew the line occasionally. "Quenelle show was absolutely marvelous," one of them wrote to her after seeing the program. In it Julia ground fillets of fish, mixed the fish with a cream puff batter, beat in dollop after dollop of cream until the mixture was holding as much cream as it possibly could without becoming too loose to handle, then shaped the mixture into cylinders and poached them—a fairly intense series of procedures, with pitfalls lying in wait around every corner. "Very very interesting watching the process and all quite clear," Julia's friend complimented her. "Would never make them in the living world." Neither would most of the other fans in the audience, but that didn't stop them from heading for the television when it was time for Julia every week. Quenelles weren't necessarily the point. "We love to watch you cook—myself especially—with your mouth-watering recipes—positively *'Smell' them cooking!* Delicious—I'll bet!" wrote a viewer. "You sure make them sound that way as well as *look*—and best of all you are not afraid to taste as you cook—to me that's cooking!"

The food was front and center, the food was glorious; but to this letter writer and to Julia herself, *The French Chef* was about life in the kitchen. Julia didn't see any difference between French food and American food that couldn't be bridged with cooking lessons, though her idea of what belonged in a cookery class went considerably deeper than recipes and techniques. At the heart of every one of her television programs was a lesson—sometimes spoken outright and sometimes simply clear from the way she worked—about how to approach any task in the kitchen. It didn't matter whether you were planning to boil an egg or to spend the next two days making a galantine of turkey, the lesson was the same, and it was a moral template for American cooks. Use all your senses, all the time, Julia instructed. Take pains with the work; do it carefully. Relish the details. Enjoy your hunger. And remember why you're there.

Julia's own kitchen in Cambridge, Massachusetts, where she lived for more than forty years and taped three television series, officially became a national treasure in 2001. Julia turned eighty-nine that year, and as she was clearing out the house in preparation for a long-planned move to a Santa Barbara, California, retirement complex, the Smithsonian Institution put in a request for her kitchen. Julia agreed; and a team of curators and conservators quickly descended on the house to inventory everything in the kitchen, including the knives and pot holders, the dime-store vegetable peelers, and the warnings she stuck to the wall about using the garbage disposal (BEWARE ONION SKINS). Then they disassembled and transported the entire room to the National Museum of American History in Washington, D.C., where they put it back together. Apart from a new etched-acrylic window standing in for the Peg-Board where she hung copper pots and pans—the Peg-Board and copper had been promised earlier to COPIA, the American Center for Wine, Food & the Arts, in Napa, California—the kitchen was erected in the museum exactly as it had been in Cambridge. The Garland stove, the twenty-four refrigerator magnets, the plastic venetian blinds, the big wooden table, the copper stockpot full of rolling pins, her phone and her *Bulfinch's Mythology* and her guide to Massachusetts state government—it was all in place. Julia's kitchen had moved from her home to our history.

Her talent was cooking and her medium was food, but all the signals radiating from Julia as she sliced potatoes or carefully unmolded a dessert had to do with character. All of her fans understood this. They responded to her generous nature and abundant skills, maybe even tried to make their own puff pastry, because they knew they could believe in her. She wasn't selling them anything; on the contrary, she was giving them everything. "Be sure to taste it at this point, because it's perfectly delicious," she advised in the course of making *riz à l'impératrice.* "It's an experience of pure vanilla and sugar and tender rice"—here she raised the spoon to her lips, closed her eyes, fixed her attention for a moment wholly on flavor, and then lifted her gaze—"that you shouldn't miss, because that's one of the nice things about being the cook." She always tasted, not just to get the flavors right, but for the incomparable pleasure of the encounter.

CONTENTS

Chapter 1

Hungry

JULIA RARELY turned down a request for an interview, and one of the questions that came up frequently over the years was about the food she remembered from childhood. What did she eat growing up? What turned her into a cook, a gourmand, a tireless advocate of the kitchen as the most important room in the house? She never had much to say on the subject. "It was good, plain New England food, the kind my mother had back in Massachusetts," she once told *People* magazine. The meat was invariably cooked until well done, she recalled; the vegetables were seasonal; in those days, of course, there was no wine. The family always employed a cook, and only on her night out would Julia's mother step into the kitchen to make baking powder biscuits and Welsh rarebit. These were the memories Julia scraped from a dry well. The truth was, food hadn't been important to her when she was growing up. She was not a natural epicure, one of those food lovers who seem to remember every childhood meal all the way back to that first, transcendent mouthful of strained peaches. And she certainly wasn't a natural cook—her calamitous efforts to learn her way around a kitchen would go on for years. What she did have was a huge, unstoppable appetite. Tall and skinny, she plowed through the first several decades of her life with only one gastronomic thought—"To eat all she could hold at every meal," as her husband put it. Food would not take on any greater significance than that until she was thirty-two years old, thousands of miles from home, and falling in love.

Julia's mother used to say that she had raised eighteen feet of children, for each of her three—Julia, Dorothy, and John—eventually topped six feet. Julia was the oldest, a gawky youngster who liked riding her bike, acting in school plays, building treehouses, and trying to smoke cigars in the orchard. Pasadena, where she was born in 1912, was a handsome city known for its wealth and civic accomplishments; and her father, John McWilliams, was a living symbol of the city's prosperity. A Princeton graduate and devout Republican, he managed the western landholdings and investments amassed by his own father, and later became vice president of the J. G. Boswell Company, one of California's major landowners and developers. His personal and professional mission was to keep California booming, and he put a great deal of time into Pasadena community life. Julia was raised to admire his discipline and public spirit, which she did, but he also nurtured a set of rabidly right-wing convictions that she would come to abhor. The two of them split sharply during the 1950s, when John McWilliams became an enthusiastic supporter of Senator Joseph McCarthy, whom Julia found despicable. Her father was also vocal about his contempt for Jews, artists, intellectuals, and foreigners; and for most of her adult life Julia viewed him with enormous dismay, though she managed to keep loving him.

Her mother was a very different creature, lively and full of humor, and Julia adored her. Julia Carolyn Weston, known as Caro, grew up in a wealthy household of seven children in Dalton, Massachusetts—her father founded the Weston Paper Company and made a fortune—and Caro developed a streak of cheerful independence she never lost. She went to Smith College in nearby Northampton, where she was a star of track and basketball, and so loved the place that she and a classmate vowed they would send their daughters there. The early death of her mother was a sorrow that Caro felt for the rest of her life, and she blamed her father for the nonstop childbearing she believed had badly weakened her mother. Julia would be childless herself, to her regret, but she made Planned Parenthood her favorite charity.

For all their pride in Pasadena, Julia's parents sent her out of town for high school so she could attend the best school they knew—the Katharine Branson School in Marin County, where Julia became a boarder. Small, expensive, and very highly regarded, the Branson School offered West Coast girls a traditional New England education, the sort that would prepare them for Seven Sisters colleges. It was largely wasted on Julia. Her work was good enough to get her by without trouble, but what she really liked about the school was everything else, including beach parties, hiking expeditions, innumerable athletic events, and playing the title role in *Michael, the Sword Eater.* She won an armful of awards at graduation in honor of her accomplishments and school spirit, and was named Branson's First Citizen. There was no question about what would follow Branson: her mother had been waiting eighteen years to help Julia pack for Smith. Many years later, Julia remarked that if she had known about such things as coed colleges, she would have raced to one. But at the time, luckily for family harmony, she had no such ambitions; in fact, she had few ambitions of any sort. Filling out an enrollment form that asked her to list vocational plans, she wrote, "No occupation decided; Marriage preferable." The next four years passed in a romp, interspersed with only enough studying to keep her from getting bored. She majored in history, though looking back, even she couldn't say why. Her prom dates tended to be family friends, since she towered over most of the eligible men at nearby Amherst College; and by the time she graduated, she was no closer to marriage, much less an "occupation," than she had been when she enrolled.

Back in Pasadena she spent a year doing exactly what her friends were doing—parties, golf, Junior League, and going to weddings. Then she took herself in hand and decided it was time to become a novelist or maybe find a job in publishing. She took a stenography course and moved to New

York with two of her Smith friends, settling into an apartment on East 59th Street in the fall of 1935. To her consternation, she couldn't get an interview at *The New Yorker*, and she flunked the entry-level typing test at *Newsweek*, so she was proud and relieved to be hired in the advertising department at W. & J. Sloane, a Fifth Avenue furniture store.

For the next year and a half, she supplied New York newspapers with press releases on Sloane's new products. Julia was no furniture expert, but she was a quick study, and she did like to write. "When you have put your all into a party, and struggled over making sandwiches that are chic and dashing as well as tastey [*sic*], it is terribly deflating to have their pretty figures ruined by guests who must peak [*sic*] inside each 'wich to see what it's made of," ran the draft of one effort. The Sloane solution was "sandwich indicators"—"wooden picks which you stick in the sandwich plate, nicely shaped and painted. There is 'Humpty-Dumpty' for egg, a rat in a cage for cheese, a dog, boat, and pig for meat, fish, and ham. And it seems like a very sound idea." That last sentence has the ring of desperation: even Julia couldn't come up with more to say about the charm of identifying a cheese sandwich with a rat.

She was writing and getting paid for it—$20 a week, eventually raised to $35—but the appeal of Sloane's and New York didn't last very long. By the end of her first year in the city, she had fallen in love, which was thrilling, and been jilted, which was shattering. She stuck it out until May 1937 and then went back to Pasadena.

Shortly after she returned home, her mother died at sixty of complications stemming from high blood pressure. Her father wanted Julia to stay near him, so she obediently narrowed her focus to a life at home. When the Smith vocational office alerted her to job possibilities in New York and Paris, she ignored them. Instead, she took a stab at fashion writing, becoming a columnist for a new and painfully obscure California magazine called *Coast.* She got the job through family connections and worked hard at it, reporting on the latest styles and suggesting what to wear with what; but the fact was, the woman who would become famous wearing a skirt, a blouse, an apron, and a dish towel really did not care what people wore with what. "Loathesome business," she called her fashion career years later; and she was relieved when the magazine went bankrupt. The Beverly Hills branch of W. & J. Sloane then made her its advertising manager, a new position at the store and one with considerable responsibility—she set up the office, managed a $100,000 annual budget, and planned and carried out all the advertising for the store—but she was fired after a few months. "I don't wonder," she wrote candidly on her résumé. "One needs a much more detailed knowledge of business . . . than I had."

Her social and volunteer activities were far more successful: she gave lots of parties and poured tremendous energy into the Junior League, writing children's plays and sometimes acting in them, and contributing to the league's magazine. She was even courted by an eligible suitor—

Harrison Chandler, a member of the family who owned the *Times-Mirror.* Julia was tempted, but decided she just didn't love him. The prerequisites for marriage, in her view, were "companionship, interests, great respect, and fun," and the relationship with Chandler didn't measure up. By this time, she was nearing thirty and starting to see that she might not marry at all. With the equanimity that would guide her all her life through crises large and small, she absorbed that possibility and kept right on going.

But she changed direction. As she started to envision life as a single woman, she realized she had no wish to spend the rest of her years as a Pasadena socialite. In the fall of 1941, caught up in the news of impending war, she began volunteering at the local office of the Red Cross. After Pearl Harbor, she joined the Aircraft Warning Service and then took the civil service exam. She was becoming increasingly impatient with life at home. A crisis was sweeping the globe, and for the past five years she had been doing little more than enjoying herself. Now the nation needed everyone—for once, even women were being called to serve. Here was a rare opening in the sky-high wall of convention and family responsibility that normally barred women from the world at large. Like millions of others, Julia leaped to take advantage. She filled out applications to join the Waves and the Wacs and set out eagerly for Washington, D.C. There she learned to her disappointment that at six feet two inches she was too tall for the military. So she took the only war-effort job she could get—typing index cards at the U.S.

Information Center in the Office of Wartime Intelligence. It was unbearably tedious. She quit after three months with no idea about what would come next, but never for a minute did she contemplate returning home. Her departure from the past was permanent. The war offered her a future, and she grabbed it.

"I got an awfully late start," Julia reflected once. She wasn't talking about marrying at thirty-four, or beginning her life's work at thirty-seven, or launching a television career at fifty. The start she had in mind was the moment when her childhood finally ended and she could feel herself coming into focus as the person she wanted to be. It happened during the war, in the heat and stress of a military office rigged up on a Ceylon tea plantation. Later, when she looked back at this turning point, she could hardly believe she had spent so long in a foreign country—and she didn't mean Ceylon, she meant Pasadena.

What she really wanted to do in Washington was join the newly formed Office of Strategic Services (OSS), headed by General William "Wild Bill" Donovan, who was organizing what would become a far-flung network of espionage and intelligence operations in Europe and the Far East. It's not clear whether Julia hoped to become a spy—she wasn't exactly someone who could fade imperceptibly into a crowd—but by this time she was a master at typing and filing, and her background made her just the sort of woman Donovan was trying to hire. An OSS recruiter once said that Donovan's concept of the ideal office worker was "a cross between a Smith College graduate, a Powers model, and a Katie Gibbs secretary." Julia fit the template nicely. She started as a file clerk at OSS headquarters, but as soon as word went out that Donovan was establishing bases overseas and was looking for volunteers, she put her name forward. Although she knew some French and a bit of Italian, she didn't ask for a posting in Europe. When the war was over, she would surely get there on her own and maybe even live abroad for a time. In hopes of just such a possibility, she was already taking French lessons three times a week. But here was a chance to travel someplace completely improbable, someplace way, way off the map of her life to date. She requested India and sailed on a troop ship from California in March 1944.

Once they all arrived—a flock of men and a handful of women—their orders changed. The new OSS base was to be in Ceylon, where Admiral Lord Louis Mountbatten was directing the South East Asia Command from Kandy, up in the hills. "Our office is a series of palm-thatched huts connected by cement walks, surrounded by native workmen and barbed wire," Julia wrote to her family from the tea plantation that became OSS headquarters. Though she had an emergency signaling mirror and felt quite ready for attack or capture, her job turned out to be chiefly paperwork. Julia's assignment was to set up and operate the Registry, a massive chore that she did single-handedly until an assistant showed up months later. The Registry handled all the highly classified documents pertaining to intelligence in the China-Burma-India theater, and Julia created the system that would keep track of every scrap of information and make it quickly accessible.

There were insects the likes of which she had never seen before, elephants and tropical rains, golf games and a huge workload—Julia thrived on all of it. Primitive living conditions didn't bother her, and she was calm about dealing with the vital wartime secrets that flowed in and out of her office. When the OSS shifted operations to China ten months later, Julia was transferred to Kunming to set up the Registry there. By now she was getting tired of a daily life devoted to paperwork, but she liked the idea of seeing another new country, and not even the famously treacherous flight over the Himalayas upset the genial self-possession that was a hallmark of her personality. One of her OSS colleagues remembered sitting on the plane from Calcutta to Kunming as it rattled through ice and wind—hundreds of flights on this route ended disastrously—while the people around her shook with fear. Not Julia; she was absorbed in a book. When they reached the airport, she looked around with pleasure and remarked, "It looks *just* like China."

Julia had what they used to call a good war. She spent it in a world she had barely known existed, and the exotic locales were the least of it. What seized her imagination most were her colleagues, the vigorous academics and professionals Donovan had made a point of recruiting. She had grown up with people who had money, leisure, and every opportunity for travel and education, yet who spent their lives absorbed in golf and parties—a class she later described as "a lot of Old Republicans with blinders on, and women who rarely develop out of the child class and create just about nothing." Now, in the excitement and heightened intimacy of wartime, she was meeting people who saw the world very differently. Here were "missionaries, geographers, anthropologists, psychiatrists, ornithologists," people who had chosen work they loved and pursued it with hearts and minds fully engaged. They spoke foreign languages, they were eager to taste foreign foods, they were passionate, sophisticated, and adventurous. Her mind flew open. She had found her tribe.

Back at the Branson School, in her senior year, Julia had published a witty essay in the literary magazine that began "I am like a cloud." She was born, she wrote, with deficient tear glands, which meant that at the slightest emotional stimulus her eyes began to flood. Sitting in the theater she tended to embarrass everyone around her. Yet this did not mean she was a maudlin creature, she emphasized, far from it. She might look weepy and vulnerable, "but in my innermost inner I am as hard as a nail!"

No, she wasn't hard as a nail, at school or later. The warmth she projected was genuine. But Julia had a firmness at the core, a constitutional strength of spirit that helped her pass smoothly through her first thirty years without the trauma or self-pity that might have attacked another woman in the same situation. She was always too tall to receive the abundant romantic attentions that someone with her charm had every right to expect; she was ruefully aware that she had wasted most of the time she spent at Smith; she had flubbed both her dream career as a writer and her actual career in business; and her single status at age thirty was like a medal of dishonor proclaiming inadequate femininity. None of this forced her psyche into neurotic twists and turns. Julia could not be toppled: there wasn't an ounce of self-destruction in her personality, and her confidence ran so deep she hardly noticed it. But she knew that Donovan's office had been her salvation, and that the war years put her on a road she might never have located otherwise. She always kept her OSS signaling mirror in a kitchen drawer.

The most important person she encountered in Ceylon was the man who would make her Julia Child. The two of them became friends right away, since Julia attracted friends as naturally as she laughed. Apart from her sociability and her impressive skills at the Registry, however, Paul Child found few points of contact with this big, jovial Californian. It wasn't so much that their backgrounds were different—nobody had a background like Paul's—but that Julia still seemed embedded in hers. Raised carefully in a manner befitting her parents' comfortable ambitions for her, she was naive and inexperienced—a "grown-up-little-girl," Paul thought. He, by contrast, had lived like a character in a boys' adventure story. His father, who worked in the Astrophysical Observatory at the Smithsonian, had died in 1902, when Paul and his twin brother, Charlie, were only a few months old. Their mother, Bertha Cushing Child, moved the two boys and their sister back to Boston, where she had grown up. A trained contralto, she managed to support the family by teaching and performing, and received good reviews for her appearances with the Boston Symphony Orchestra and the Handel and Haydn Society. Meanwhile, the boys studied violin and cello, and their sister took piano lessons. As soon as they could all manage their instruments, Bertha booked the quartet for salon performances as "Mrs. Child and the Children." Music was only the first of Paul's numerous careers. After high school he worked in a stained-glass shop, learning to cut and glaze, and then he headed out west. Over the next few decades, he was a waiter in Hollywood, a tutor for an American family in Italy, a woodcarver in Paris, and a teacher at a couple of private schools in New England. Along the way he acquired a black belt in judo and became an avid photographer, painter, gardener, and poet. At the OSS he worked in the visual presentation unit, which prepared maps, charts, and graphic displays, and he was setting up the war room in Kandy when he met Julia on the veranda of the tea plantation.

Setting up war rooms was exactly the sort of thing Paul did best. In fact, he would do it many times in his life with Julia, organizing her high-performance kitchens at home and in the television studio. He was passionately analytical and took deep pleasure in trying to pin down the unwieldy universe in images, designs, and language. One of the many subjects that fascinated him was general semantics, a philosophy of language that he studied for years. Followers of general semantics, which emphasized the perpetually inexact relation between words and things, were fond of the abbreviation *etc.*, because it implied that however much had been expressed, there was always something left unsaid. Paul tried to say it, all of it. He wrote constantly to his brother, Charlie, page after page of graceful calligraphy describing his days, his thinking, and his work with such dedication that he might have been the Homer of his own lifelong odyssey.

Paul was largely unsentimental, but his emotional life was always in full gear, and during the war years, he was deeply absorbed in the problem of women. He had lived for seventeen years, in Paris and in Cambridge, Massachusetts, with a woman named Edith Kennedy, who was some twenty years older than he. Widely accomplished, brilliant, and sophisticated, Kennedy had died of cancer in 1942. Three years later, Paul was still longing hopelessly for her. "I am really spoiled for other women and I realize it over and over," he wrote mournfully to Charlie. Before he left the United States, an astrologer in whom he put considerable faith had revealed his future to him. "Sometime after April 1945" was the predicted time frame; at that point he could expect to fall in love with a woman who would be, according to the astrologer, "intelligent, dramatic, beautiful, a combination of many facets, can keep house, yet is a modern woman." By the spring of 1945, Paul was lonely, grieving, sexually deprived, and waiting impatiently for the prediction to come true.

There certainly were enough candidates. Was it Nancy, code-named Zorina in his letters? Zorina was the name he and Charlie gave to certain women who physically resembled the famous ballet dancer while exuding a kind of essential female quality that greatly appealed to both twins. "They possess what is lacking in this warring, man-ridden world: a sense of the continuity of life and perpetual sympathy, fellow-feeling and consolation," Paul once said about their Zorinas. But Nancy was in love with another man, and Paul finally gave up on her. Perhaps Janie? "*Une Bohémienne,* of a fine sort. She adores animals and people, draws with great style and is worldly and often witty. She speaks Malay and French, both well." But it didn't last. "The woman could be Rosamond," he wrote excitedly. "No Zorina she, but a wonderfully interesting and *alive* person, speaking French and Chinese and in spite of a woman-hockey-player's figure, very attractive physically." But Rosie was in her twenties and too young to be very interesting for very long. "When am I going to meet a grown-up dame with beauty, brains, character, sophistication, and sensibility?" he exclaimed in agony. Finally, she appeared—Marjorie, definitely Marjorie. "She has a first class brain and is widely informed, is wonderfully quick, subtle and humorous, but very earnest about life and its problems and possibilities. You begin to love women like that the moment you see them, almost." But Marjorie went off with someone else.

This barrage of failure, and the possibility of spending the rest of his life alone, prompted a bleak poem.

These prison-wires strung round my bones
Bear cryptic messages from the heart.

Wasteland, wasteland—never a bush—
No gushing coolness under the rock,
Devoid of butterfly and buttercup.

Vacant as an idiot's eye.

These pipes, pulsing in my flesh,
Water no garden, fertilize no flower.

Bitter, bitter on the sand is love.
Love lost, love never gained, love unfulfilled.
The teeming world is lonely as a mooreland,
As a bird in the middle of the sea.

Meanwhile, there was Julia, who impressed him chiefly by virtue of her good nature and great legs. Three months after they met, he sent a photo of her to Charlie, devoting more of the letter to a description of the bunk room than to the woman in it. Lying on a cot, stretched out to her full, dramatic length, Julia wore a dress and pearls, lipstick, and nail polish. She was leaning on an elbow, with one long leg angled over the other in a manner that suggests she was trying, somewhat against nature, to look coy. "The enclosed photo is of Julia, the 6'2" bien-jambée from Pasadena," wrote Paul. "The room is a typical 10' x 18' with its coir matting, woven cadjan walls, wooden shutters and army bed with folded-up mosquito net above." He added, "Save the photo for me please," but it's not clear whether it was Julia he hoped to preserve or his careful documentation of the room. Later he wrote out a detailed analysis of his new friend, making it clear why she would never qualify as the woman of his dreams. "Her mind is potentially good, but she is an extremely sloppy thinker," he told Charlie, blaming Julia's well-cushioned background for her inability to observe life in any depth or nuance. "She says things like this, 'I don't see why the Indians don't just throw out the British,' and 'I can't understand what they see in that horrid little old Gandhi.'" It's easy even now to imagine Julia voicing these comments. Bluntness was a trait she would retain for the rest of her life; and whether or not she knew what she was talking about, her inclination was to speak out and accept the consequences. What saved her from being narrow-minded was an ingrained habit of trying out new ideas and perspectives. She was always eager to learn and rarely clung to a belief just because it was familiar. Paul's take on her thinking was incomplete, but it was accurate for 1944; and he would be the one responsible for igniting her intellect.

For Julia, falling in love with Paul was a cinch, in part because she had already fallen in love, headlong and forever, with the whole OSS team and what it stood for in the way of civilized living. Paul was the very emblem of these new values. His sophistication dazzled her, easily outweighing the fact that he was ten years older, considerably shorter, and sported a mustache that suited him poorly. Just as important, Paul liked women a lot, and he was completely comfortable with strong, capable females—even strong, capable females who towered over him. Julia was sexually shy, but she was hardly unwilling, and she found Paul's experience a very desirable asset. Here was a man who plainly relished all his physical appetites, and she responded as if the power had been switched on inside her. To be hungry for food was a state she knew well. To be hungry all over was a revelation. Nothing and nobody in her wondrous new environment resembled her stodgy past, Paul least of all. She had to have this.

It took a good eighteen months. Paul found Julia "*extremely* likeable and pleasant to have around," but he had no intention of pursuing her romantically. She was a virgin, he reported to Charlie, and probably afraid of sex—a state that did not appeal to Paul at all. Here, he decided, was "the traditional old maid of song and story," subconsciously obsessed with sex but unable to handle the reality. "I feel very sorry for her because while I see clearly what the cure is, I do not see clearly who will apply it," he wrote. "I have considered the matter carefully, as obviously there would be compensations and pleasures, but I believe the lack of worldly knowledge, the sloppy thinking, the wild emotionalism, the conventional framework, would be too much for Dr. Paulski to risk attempting to cure." What's more, he was irritated by her most prominent speech mannerisms. "She has a slight atmosphere of hysteria which gets on my nerves, being given to overstress in conversation and to gasping when she talks excitedly," he told Charlie—habits he would come to love as her public did. But at the time, they simply contributed to the many reasons why Julia fell short of his ideal.

So they embarked on a friendship, nothing more. Julia was out of the running. "I have never liked the idea—which is so appealing to many men—of Man the Sculptor, moulding and shaping a woman to his desire," Paul explained to his brother, never imagining that love itself might be a sculptor pretty handy with clay. He and Julia went to movies, traveled a bit in Ceylon, and when she was transferred to China shortly after he was, they did some sightseeing there as well. They shared many meals; they talked and talked. And often they talked about food. Paul had spent years in Paris and was a knowledgeable and enthusiastic food lover. Julia liked these conversations—she certainly liked them better than the ones about general semantics—but as far as she was concerned, the most delicious thing about the meals they shared was Paul. Nonetheless, her sharp intellect rooted around happily in the talk about flavors, recipes, and culinary cultures that flowed between herself and this entrancing man. Paul was quickly persuaded that he had met a fellow epicure. "She is a gourmet and likes to cook and talk about food," he reported admiringly, a few months after meeting her. He also knew a great deal about music, which she found less of a stretch, since she had minored in the subject at Smith. ("She is *devoted* to music," Paul told Charlie approvingly.) Her shortcomings were, of course, severe in his eyes. But he came to treasure the qualities she brought to a friendship—constancy, humor, resilience, character. About six months after they met: "Julia is a nice person, a warm and witty girl." Several months later: "A darling warm lovely girl." A year after they met: "Julie . . . is a great solace." And at last, in August 1945, a sonnet for her birthday. This was only three months after he had written the poem beginning "These prison-wires strung round my bones," with its despairing imagery of the wasteland and the lonely sea. Now he was in full Shakespearean mode, and it was Julia's doing.

How like the Autumn's warmth is Julia's face
So filled with Nature's bounty, Nature's worth.
And how like summer's heat is her embrace
Wherein at last she melts my frozen earth.
Endowed, the awakened fields abound
With newly green effulgence, smiling flowers.
Then all the lovely riches of the ground
Spring up, responsive to her magic powers.
Sweet friendship, like the harvest-cycle, moves
From scattered seed to final ripened grain,
Which, glowing in the warmth of Autumn, proves

The richness of the soil, and mankind's gain.
I cast this heaped abundance at your feet
An offering to Summer, and her heat.

Still, they weren't quite engaged when the war ended. For all the delights of this relationship, they both worried that perhaps it was just a wartime fling. Maybe what Julia called their "friendly passion," which was rooted in their great enjoyment of each other's company, wasn't powerful enough to see them through to marriage and beyond. Julia was painfully aware of how different she was from Paul's great love, Edith Kennedy, who had been chic, intellectual, and—Paul's favorite term of approval—"worldly." Years later, when they were married and living in Paris, she could go to a Christian Dior fashion show and admire the "slightly ravaged 'worldly' look" of the models, admitting it was a look far beyond her power to achieve. ("Great big milk-fed 'femme de menage,' that's me.") But now she just had to hope it wasn't an insurmountable problem. As they parted in China with plans to meet each other's family and test the relationship by the light of real life, neither one knew quite what would come next. Julia went back to Pasadena, and Paul returned to Washington and the State Department. They spent the first six months of 1946 on opposite coasts, writing letters and pondering the future. And, as it turned out, missing each other terribly. If this was "friendly passion," the emphasis was beginning to fall equally on both terms. "I am in a warm love-lust mood, wanting to have my ear-rings eaten," she sighed, having just received two letters and a packet of photos from "Paulski." For his part, he said he wanted to "see you, touch you, kiss you, talk with you, eat with you . . . eat you, maybe. I have a Julie-need."

Julia knew she didn't want to settle in Pasadena, no matter what happened with Paul, but she couldn't figure out what to do with herself. By now she was sick of filing and secretarial work, yet she hadn't come home from the war with any more specific career plans than she had when she left. What she really wanted to do was marry Paul, but she could hardly explain that to him, so she wrote to him about her plans in carefully circumspect fashion. Maybe she ought to look for a job in Hollywood? "I don't know, as I have no contacts yet," she mused. "I feel that it is not worth it to me to get any kind of a job like 'Registry,' nor a job that doesn't pay at least $4,000 a year. I want something in which I will grow, meet many people and many situations. There is also and always Washington and the gov't—both of which I like."

But it was clear, at least to Julia, that the real project for her stay in Pasadena was to work on becoming Mrs. Paul Child, a project somehow distinct from the question of if and when they would marry. Marriage was inconceivable unless Paul found her to be the right person, and she knew she wasn't, yet. She had no wish to give up her identity; what she was hoping to do was expand it to meet his, and then dissolve the borders. Paul urged her to read Henry

Miller, which she did with mixed reactions (magnificent writing, she thought, but too much of a "stiff-prick forest"); she also took up semantics, psychology, and politics, which she followed in the *Washington Post* and the *New York Times.* "There is just *so much* that is fascinating!" she told him, and underlined the phrase eight times. When she turned to cooking, it was in the same frame of mind—here was an exhilarating intellectual adventure that would bring her closer to Paul. Cooking, love, and learning would be conjoined for the rest of her life.

And learning—conscientious, painstaking, step-by-step learning—was at the center of the enterprise from the moment she first propped a cookbook on the counter and went to work. Julia had none of the instincts that make a man or a woman "a born cook." Much as she enjoyed food, it's unlikely that her cooking would have acquired much depth or refinement on its own. She simply wasn't one of those mysteriously gifted creatures who could wander into the kitchen and wander out again bearing a wonderful meal, never having glanced at a recipe or measured an ingredient. Cookbooks were supposed to help, and she studied them with the faith and zeal of a Torah scholar; but the recipes always seemed to fall horribly short. One day she made a broiled chicken according to the directions in a book, checked on it when the book said to, and found a blackened mess. If she was going to cook, and cook well enough to please Paul, she knew she needed lessons.

Two British women, Mary Hill and Irene Radcliffe, ran

the Hillcliff School of Cookery in Beverly Hills; and in the spring of 1946, Julia started going three times a week. She was ambitious and diligent, but when she came home with her new knowledge and put it into practice, nothing seemed to happen as it should. A dish of brains turned into mush on the stove, a duck blew up in the oven because she forgot to prick the skin. She mastered béarnaise sauce—"Awfully easy when the tricks are known," she told Paul airily—but tried it another time using lard instead of butter and watched the whole thing congeal into a vile mass. There were triumphs occasionally: she and a friend gave an elaborate dinner for twelve featuring three kinds of hors d'oeuvres, steak and kidney pie ("The crust was superb"), and peas cooked with lettuce, the French way. But then there was the day she got up at 6:30 in the morning to make the family a big breakfast and ended up in near-hysterics two hours later when she still hadn't managed to put any food on the table. "The kitchen was a mess, and they came in and hovered over me, and the coffee fell on the floor and burned them, and they made rude remarks, and I threw them out and burst into tears," she recalled years later, still grim at the memory.

Julia wrote to Paul about all of it, whether the results were delicious or disastrous. Far more than books or politics, food became a red-hot connective wire between them during these months of separation, a living metaphor for the intimacy that had seemed so elusive at the end of the war. "I feel I am only existing until I see you, and hug you, and eat you," Julia wrote; and Paul suggested that she move to Washington and become his cook—"We can eat each other." This was the highly charged context in which Julia threw herself into studying recipes, practicing her Hillcliff lessons, and staging dinner parties: every cup of flour and sprinkle of herbs seemed to radiate her desire for Paul. He, too, was getting hungry. In July, he showed up in Pasadena, and the two of them got into Julia's Buick and drove back across the country together.

It was the supreme test: long, hot days on the road, nights in cheap motels. Julia had packed eight bottles of whiskey, a bottle of gin, and a bottle of premixed martinis. She was as good a driver as Paul, he noted with approval, and it turned out that they liked stopping to look at all the same things—"wineries, crab-canneries, local architecture and nature." Julia never complained, ate and slept as comfortably as if she were traveling in luxury, painted her toenails, and washed Paul's shirts. "Quite a dame," he told Charlie. By the time they reached Niagara Falls, he was in love and knew it.

Julia's determination had carried her to a glorious finish line: the raw, emotionally chaotic "old maid" that Paul once dismissed was now his lodestar. Sitting down to analyze his rush of awakened feelings in a letter to his brother, Paul tried to figure out what had happened. Did Julia change, or did he? It was Julia, he decided. And Julia had indeed changed, or rather she had opened up areas of her mind and personality that nobody before Paul had demanded to see. Yet when he went on to list what he loved most about her, he didn't dwell on the intellectual skills that had newly flowered, but rather on the great, stalwart elements of her character that had always made people warm to her—and would have the same effect years later on millions of people she would never meet. "She *never* puts on an act," he wrote, pinpointing at the top of the roster the very quality her audiences would relish most. "She frankly likes to eat and use her senses and has an unusually keen nose. . . . She has a cheerful, gay humor with considerable gusto. . . . She loves life and all its phenomena. . . . She has deep-seated charm and human warmth which I have been fascinated to see at work on people of all sorts, from the sophisticates of San Francisco to the mining and cattle folk of the Northwest . . . She tells the truth." And he noted appreciatively that she had none at all of the "measly Mrs. Grundyisms concerning sex" that might have been expected in an inexperienced woman nearly thirty-four years old. A month later, they were married.

Chapter 2

Prof. Julia

THE STORY OF Julia Child's first meal in France has been told and retold, most eloquently by Julia herself. In 1948, she and Paul were living in Washington, not quite sure of where his career was heading, when to their great joy the State Department posted him to Paris to become exhibits officer at the United States Information Service (USIS). They arrived at Le Havre on November 3, and as soon as their Buick emerged from the ship, they drove off toward the capital. Around lunchtime they came to Rouen. The name of the restaurant was La Couronne, and Paul—"in his beautiful French," Julia recalled—ordered the meal. She described it lovingly in the fish chapter of *From Julia Child's Kitchen:* first came oysters and Chablis, and then a splendid sole *meunière* was set before them. "It was handsomely browned and still sputteringly hot under its coating of chopped parsley, and around it swirled a goodly amount of golden Normandy butter," Julia wrote. "It was heaven to eat, the flesh so very fresh, with its delicate yet definite texture and taste that blended marvelously with the browned butter sauce. I was quite overwhelmed." This traditional dish, each detail put into place with care and all of it glorious with butter, had everything she would always adore about French cooking. She published the memory in 1975, and in time it joined Swann dipping his madeleine, and M. F. K. Fisher drying tangerines on the radiator, as a classic of culinary nostalgia.

Twelve years later, Julia wrote again about her first meal in France. In an essay she contributed to a book of Christmas food memories she described the same Buick, the same arrival in Rouen, the same restaurant—but a different menu. "We started with oysters, followed with one of their famous duck dishes," she wrote. "While husband Paul commandeered a fat ripe Comice pear for dessert and an equally fat wedge of Camembert, I went for the pastries." No sole *meunière*? Who knows? Most likely she'd forgotten the earlier version. And even the earlier version may have been conflated with other cherished menus. Paul, who described their first meal in France in a letter written from Paris to his brother that very day, said they had blissfully eaten oysters ("*very* strong of the sea") and *filet de sole,* without specifying the preparation. But sole, especially *meunière,* came up again and again in his accounts of restaurant meals during those heady first weeks—"Julie had a delicious sole *meunière,*" "Julie can't get over how good the sole is," "Julie wants to spend the rest of her life right here, eating sole." Julia, too, wrote home about it: "Sole *meunière,* crisp and bristling from the fire." Plainly, that simple homage to freshness and butter made an impression on her. As for the "famous duck" of Rouen, it's not clear how this particular dish made its way into her official past; but Julia loved storytelling, and she loved duck; maybe she had one roasting in the oven while she was typing that day. In 2000, she was asked to describe her "most memorable meal" for *Gourmet*, and once more she gazed back happily to Le Havre, to the Buick, to the restaurant in Rouen, and to the duck—"fire-roasted and then passed through a duck press." What emerges from these memories, one folded into another and all of them touched with sepia, is the staying power of the encounter itself, which began when the ship docked and continued for months in a haze of rapture. The rapture was the part she never forgot, and never revised.

Soon after Julia and Paul settled in Paris, an old woman told Julia that France was "just one big family." As far as Julia was concerned, that family was hers. At their favorite restaurant, Michaud, she couldn't stop glancing over at a dozen people celebrating around a table spread with "innumerable courses of everything"—champagne, chickens, salads, cheeses, nuts—and everyone relaxed and good-hearted as they talked and ate and drank. "We keep being reminded of the Orient," she wrote home. "Possibly because both are cultivated old civilizations, who enjoy and have integrated the physical and the cultural things in living." Julia was at home here. The French struck her as wonderfully natural and earthy, and at the same time immensely civilized. They seemed to believe that the great pleasures of life—food, drink, sex, civility and conversation, pets, children, the splendor of Paris—were simply part of the fabric of being human, and that to enjoy them was as fundamental as breathing. Yet it was also taken for granted that stewardship of these gifts meant relishing them openly, discussing them, arguing about them, and keeping them meaningful through the very power of appreciation. Here was a whole country dedicated to being "worldly." Right away she started French lessons at Berlitz: nothing was more important to her at this stage than becoming comfortable in the language. She was ecstatically absorbing the city, all her senses wide open and craving more; and she wanted the sounds as well, that constant chatter in the shops and streets; she wanted to "talk and talk and talk" and make a place for herself in the life flowing around her. "Oh, La Vie! I love it more every day."

They found an apartment at 81, rue de l'Université, on the Left Bank of the Seine across from the place de la Concorde, in an old private house. Their rooms on the third floor were as French as the view of rooftops outside the windows. Sagging leather wallpaper, gilt chairs, moldings, and mirrors everywhere—Julia called it "late 19th century Versailles." Up a narrow flight of stairs there was a roomy kitchen with appliances so small in relation to her height that she might have been standing over a toy stove. She decided she could live right there in that apartment forever, in perfect happiness. Already she regretted missing Paris in the twenties, an era Paul had seen in person; and she pounced happily on the occasional sighting of such figures as Colette, Chanel, André Gide, and Sylvia Beach. Once, when the Childs gave a Bastille Day party, Paul invited Alice B. Toklas, whom he had met back in the twenties. She arrived, drank a glass of wine, and left. Toklas was so tiny, and wore such a wide-brimmed hat, that the only way Julia could see her face was to be sitting down while Toklas stood directly above her.

Julia spent her first months studying French, walking through the streets with a map and a dictionary, and tasting, tasting, tasting. Everything she bit into was full of exhilarating flavors: the sausages, the tarts and petits fours, the snails, the Brie, "great big juicy pears," and grapes so sweet she nearly swooned. Like most of their French and American friends in Paris, she and Paul had a maid who cooked and cleaned; but after living that way for a few months, they let her go. They hated having to show up on time for meals, and her cooking disappointed them. Julia was embarrassed to serve guests such inadequate dinners—her own could be alarming at times, but when they came off well, she took a great deal of pride in them. "Besides," she wrote home, "it is heart-rending not to go to the markets, those lovely, intimate, delicious, mouth-watering, friendly, fascinating places. How can one know the guts of the city if one doesn't do one's marketing?" So they hired a cleaning woman to come in twice a week, and Julia gladly took charge of the food. At the market, she examined pigs' heads and scrutinized fruits and vegetables, breathed in the smells of the *boulangerie,* carefully chose a terrine or pâté from the charcuterie, and chatted away with the shopkeepers. In France, food was a sociable enterprise: everyone had something to say about the turnips or the kidneys, and to be able to join that nationwide conversation—in French!—was Julia's bliss.

But as the winter passed, she found she had time on her hands. She was never bored with Paris, or the daily delights of living there, but her own lack of direction bothered her. She and Paul would have liked to raise a family, but she was now thirty-six, and the possibility of children seemed increasingly remote. Surely there was something she could do professionally that would give her life substance and purpose. How about . . . hat making? She did have a bit of a background in fashion, having worked for *Coast* magazine before the war (she forgot how much she had hated the job), and Paris was certainly the capital of such things. She embarked on a few lessons and even made a dress and hat for herself that she wore to a wedding. "Awful, awful," she admitted later. Paul, too, was thinking about her problem, and he mentioned it one day to the librarian at the USIS, a Frenchman who knew Paris well. "What does Julia like?" asked the librarian. Art, perhaps? Music? Sports? Paul reflected for a moment, then said decisively, "She likes to *eat.*" He went home with the address of the Cordon Bleu.

Despite the distinction of its name and history, the Cordon Bleu had plunged into mismanagement by the time

Julia enrolled in the fall of 1949. Pots and pans went unwashed, equipment was broken, dirt was everywhere, and classes ran short of ingredients. More irritating for Julia, she found herself taking lessons with two women who had never cooked before and needed to start at the kindergarten level. After two frustrating days, she managed to get herself transferred to a professional course. Here she found eleven ex-GIs who were training to become restaurant cooks under the GI bill, and a distinguished teaching staff of master chefs long steeped in the tastes and techniques of classic French cooking. This was more like it. They started at 7:30 in the morning, Julia and the former soldiers peeling and chopping and watching and asking questions in a top-speed flurry while producing sauces, fricassees, custards, and whatever else the teachers ordered up. "It's a free-for-all," Julia told her family. "Being the only woman, I am being careful to sit back a bit, but am being very cold-blooded indeed in a quiet way (got to be cold-blooded and realistic, but retain appearance of sweetness and gentility)." At 9:30, the class was over, and Julia went home to practice on what would become lunch for herself and Paul. Then she returned to school for an afternoon demonstration class, watching intently as chefs prepared the thoroughly professional versions of soufflés, galantines, charlottes, and fondants that she planned to master. Then back to rue de l'Université, exhilarated, to make dinner. "After that one demonstration of Boeuf B, I came right home and made the most delicious one I ever ett," she wrote home jubilantly.

"My cooking has been always on the experimental side, these courses will make them SURE." She found she liked the demonstrations best, because she could learn so much from watching the chef make an entire dish from beginning to end, "giving the proportions and ingredients, and explaining everything he does, and making little remarks."

Julia's particular mentor was Chef Max Bugnard, who was seventy-four when she met him and had started his career sixty years earlier as an apprentice, later moving to London to work under Escoffier himself. Bugnard was the teacher who made Julia a cook. This generous and knowledgeable chef became a kind of culinary archetype who would rule her imagination for the rest of her life. Bugnard had a gravitas about him that came from his learning, his experience, and his respect for the work; and for Julia, such a sensibility would forever mark the difference between the real cooks and the dabblers. "He has that wonderful old-timey 'art for arts sake' approach, and nothing short of perfection satisfies him at all," she wrote to a friend. "It's an inspiration to work with such a man."

Bugnard's classes at the Cordon Bleu took place at a level far above the inadequate conditions of the school. He knew the repertoire intimately, and his standards were, as Julia often said, impeccable. As he demonstrated and explained the well-honed methods of French cookery, supervised and corrected her work, the doors she had been banging on so ineffectually swung open at last. After years of following recipes only to meet failure, enjoying a triumph only to see the same dish mysteriously go wrong the next time, planning lovely little dinners that didn't get to the table until 10:00 p.m.—now she could understand what was happening and why. Now she could learn. Julia cooked all day, all evening, and all through the weekends; and when she wasn't cooking, she was compulsively buying sieves and whisks and copper pots and larding needles. At the far end of an alley in the Paris flea market, she found a marble mortar and a pestle so massive Paul had to hoist them onto his shoulder to get them back to the car, which was parked two miles away. He was delighted to do it. "Julie's cookery is actually improving!" Paul exclaimed to his brother. "I didn't believe it would, just between us girls, but it really *is.*"

Ducks and rabbits and fish and eggs, every step of every dish, from the raw ingredients to the final garnish, everything performed by hand with only the most elemental equipment—Julia was rocketed to paradise. This was what she had needed without knowing it: a clear, rational guide to making every dish taste the way it should. No longer was she fortune's fool in the kitchen. Her mind was on fire: every day, more mysteries fell away, and in their place was structure, system, and logic. The secret behind good cooking turned out to be that there were no secrets. There was only good teaching.

Studying French cuisine wasn't just a matter of absorbing traditional rules and methods: Julia was learning to cook with all her senses engaged, to cook with a visceral understanding of raw ingredients that was increasingly out of fashion in the American kitchen. Ever since the late-nineteenth century, each generation had been purchasing more and more food that had been cleaned, cut, packaged, and sometimes partially cooked in a factory. The convenience was addictive, and so was the impressive rationale created by the advertising industry: these uniform, sterile products, "untouched by human hands" as one slogan put it, made cooking modern and far more sanitary. Why fumble around with messy, smelly chicken parts and carrot peelings the way poor Grandma had to do?

Cooking from scratch remained the standard in most households, but what women meant by "scratch" was continually changing. By the time Julia enrolled at the Cordon Bleu, an American dinner made from scratch might include beef that had been ground into hamburger before it arrived in the kitchen, bottled ketchup, fresh potatoes, canned peas, and a Jell-O dessert in the most popular flavor, namely red. In France, by contrast, to cook meant to sustain an intimate relationship with ingredients. Julia had to learn how to feel her way through a recipe even while she was following written directions, how to leave enough space from step to step to let the food itself tell her what to do next. How should the rice smell when it came out of the oven after its long baking in milk? How would the egg whites look when they had been beaten just enough? How much nutmeg would make the dish taste right—with no taste of nutmeg? She took to this approach avidly. She may have lacked the instincts of a born cook, but she was blessed with an excellent palate and skillful hands. And she loved the feel of food, loved letting her senses run riot at the kitchen counter, loved handling raw meats and vegetables and inhaling the aromas as they cooked. Learning to cook was an intoxicant; she could have been sipping her first glass of champagne. "It is beginning to take effect," she wrote home after three months at the Cordon Bleu. "I feel it in my hands, my stomach, my soul."

Yet the more she learned, the more she could see what a long way she had to go. If she were trying to play the violin, she reflected, the challenge would be the same: training and practice, training and practice. The fishmongers and butchers were nerve-rackingly good at identifying customers who didn't know what they were buying ("Bluff is no good, you've got to KNOW," she wrote home) and she was determined to "KNOW" every single thing about market and kitchen. One day she spent four hours on a lobster recipe—at the typewriter, not the stove. She had already worked on the cooking; she could prepare it just as it should be, and now she wanted to put the whole procedure into words. "Good practice, to make it absolutely exact and water-tight," she wrote the family. She did a massive round of research on mayonnaise and wrote it up in more detail than any of her sources had, then went to work on béarnaise. These mini dissertations were for herself. She wanted to have in front of her the most explicit, flawless recipes ever written, so that she would never lose touch with what she had mastered. Failure still had a horrible way of seizing control of a meal. One day, after she had been several weeks at the Cordon Bleu, she made lunch for a friend and ended up serving "the most VILE eggs Florentine I have ever imagined could be made outside of England." She didn't measure the flour, which made the sauce thick and horrid; she couldn't find spinach so she substituted chicory, and the whole mess was disgusting. Would she ever outgrow these bursts of ineptitude? Maybe not, but she wasn't about to share her guilt and misery with the guests. It was bad enough that they had to eat the stuff; they shouldn't be forced to claim it was delicious. "I carefully didn't say a word, while they painfully ate it, because I don't believe in these women who are always apologizing for their food," she wrote home. "If it is vile, the cook must just grin and bear it, with no word of excuse." Her famous advice to the hostess—"Never apologize"—was forged in crucibles like this one.

The harder she worked, the more impatient she became with her class at the Cordon Bleu. The GIs weren't making much progress, and the course was slowing down and becoming repetitive. "After 6 months, they don't know the proportions for a béchamel or how to clean a chicken the French way," she complained. Finally she decided she'd had enough of the school but not nearly enough of Bugnard, so she dropped out of the course and hired the chef to teach her privately for another six months, while she practiced between lessons. Then, with a year of study behind her, she decided she was ready to take the exam and receive a Cordon Bleu diploma. Here she ran into a problem. Madame Brassart, director of the school, had always disliked the big American woman who thought she was too good for the amateur course, pushed her way into the professional program, then dropped out before completing it. Now she had the effrontery to demand a diploma. The director refused to schedule the exam. It took months before an increasingly furious Julia was allowed to take the exam, and Madame Brassart relented only after Julia sent a letter hinting that the embassy would soon start wondering why an American student was being treated so badly by the Cordon Bleu. When Julia finally received her certificate—Madame Brassart wouldn't issue a real diploma, since Julia hadn't finished the course—it was dated March 15, 1951, some two weeks before the date on the warning letter. The director was covering her tracks. For many years, Julia included Madame Brassart on the very short list of people she hated, which was headed by Senator Joseph McCarthy.

The exam itself sorely disappointed her, for it was superficial and made no reference to the complicated procedures she had practiced with zeal. Madame Brassart had decided to give this uppity student a beginner's exam, the sort given to housewives who took a six-week elementary course. Julia was outraged, all the more so because she flubbed quite a bit of the test. She did well on the written section, in which she had to describe how to make a brown stock, how to cook green vegetables, and how to make a béarnaise sauce. But in the cooking section, she made mistakes everywhere. Asked to prepare an *oeuf mollet,* she made a poached egg instead of a soft-boiled one; she also put too much milk into the *crème renversée,* or "caramel custard," and she forgot what went into an *escalope de veau en surprise* (veal, duxelles, and sliced ham, cooked and then reheated in a paper bag). Julia sautéed the mushrooms instead of making duxelles and left out the ham entirely. "All my own fault, I just should have memorized their little book," she admitted in a letter home. "My mind was on Filets de sole Walewska, Poularde Toulousiane, Sauce Venetienne, etc. etc. etc. and I neglected to look at the primary things." Her mistakes in the paper-bag recipe didn't bother her, since it was an idiotic dish anyway—"the kind a little newlywed would serve up for her first dinner to 'épater' the boss's wife." The whole experience was frustrating: she could turn out flawless sauces, pâtés, and mousses; bone a goose without tearing the skin; clean, eviscerate, and cut up a chicken in twelve minutes—and she had tripped over her own feet when asked to take a baby step. When she opened her own cooking school, she vowed, she would turn people into cooks "through friendliness and encouragement and professionalism," not the nasty methods of the mean-spirited Madame Brassart. Who, she added pointedly, was a Belgian, and not French at all.

During these months of intensive cooking, a friend who thought Julia might like to meet another food-struck woman introduced her to Simone Beck Fischbacher—a meeting as momentous for Julia as the day she encountered Paul. Here was her first culinary soul mate and a woman who could balance Julia's classroom cuisine with real-life French home cooking. Simca, as everyone called her, had grown up in Normandy in a wealthy household with servants, but as a child she found the kitchen irresistible and soon began trying her hand. She became a brilliant, intuitive home cook, self-taught apart from a brief period of study at the Cordon Bleu, with a vast repertoire of recipes and techniques that she was continually expanding. Everything she tasted seemed to inspire her; Julia used to say she threw off ideas like a fountain. Like Julia, she was married and had no children, and cooking was at the center of her life. As soon as they were introduced, the two women started talking about French food and didn't let up until Simca's death forty years later. Their friendship, renewed year after year on the hillside in Provence where they both made second homes, launched both of their careers and spawned a huge correspondence that dissected every aspect of French cookery. They were "*ma sœur*" and "*ma grande chérie*" to each other, sisters whose volcanic arguments never quite shattered their bond. To Julia, in those early years, Simca was France itself—beloved, inspiring, wildly irritating, and fundamental to everything.

Simca belonged to a women's gastronomical club, the only one of its kind in a country where haute cuisine was a well-guarded male preserve. No women cooked or even waited on tables in the great three-star restaurants; no women were invited to join the elite dining clubs that met over grand lunches and elaborate banquets; and the most revered authorities on classic cuisine were male. Out in the provinces, of course, women did some of the most distinguished and characteristic cooking of France; and it was a reflex among chefs to honor their mothers' cooking above all other influences. But if women's cooking was the sentimental favorite, men's had the prestige, the exclusivity, and the cash value.

The lone exception to this gender divide was Le Cercle des Gourmettes, a group of food-loving women who began meeting in 1927, prompted by an incident at a sumptuous banquet held by one of the men's gastronomical societies. Women were sometimes allowed to attend these feasts as guests, and on this occasion both men and women were at the table when a man was heard declaiming the ancient truism that women, of course, understood nothing about fine food and wine. A certain Madame Ethel Ettlinger—an American who had been living for decades in France but clearly hadn't adapted—jumped up in fury to remind the men that in all their homes it was women who ran the kitchens, ordered the meals, and trained the cooks. The women then got the idea to stage a magnificent banquet of their own and invite the men. They held the dinner in a borrowed château, arranged to have each course introduced with a trumpet fanfare, and easily demonstrated that women could spend money on glorious food and wine just as knowledgeably as men could. (The women themselves didn't cook, any more than the members of the male club would have.) After that, the women chose a name for themselves and met regularly for decades, most often at an elaborate lunch prepared by a chef. Any Gourmettes who wanted to come at 10:00 a.m. to watch the chef and act as his assistants were invited to do so. Simca showed up regularly for these cooking sessions; and Julia, who joined the group soon after meeting Simca, never missed one if she could help it.

These lunches glowed in her memory long afterward. She once said they marked "the real beginning of French gastronomical life for me." The tradition she had been pursuing so ardently now sprang up before her like an edible diorama, complete with authentic chefs and guests. "I soon realized I had never really lived before," she recalled. "There was always an elegant first course, such as fresh artichoke bottoms stuffed with sweetbreads and served with a truffled Béarnaise, or a most elaborately poached fish garnished with mushroom duxelles and lobster tails, and sauced with a creamy puree of crab. The main course might be boned duck, or game in season. Then came dessert, a sorbet aux poires, garnished with pears poached in wine and served in a meringue-nut shell, or a fancy mousse, a molded Bavarian structure, or a Vacherin with exotic filling." And wines, of course, in abundance. What she liked most about the gatherings, along with the busy, gossipy cooking sessions and the dazzling food, was sitting down among women who talked food as intently as she did and ate with a gusto like her own. She was especially fond of the original members, a cluster of old-world dowagers in their seventies who dived into their lunches like ravenous teenagers. Normally Julia disliked all-female social events—she always came home grumbling afterward about how there hadn't been any men in the room—but Le Cercle was different. She had never known so many women to whom she felt kin, and she identified herself as a Gourmette with pride.

One of Simca's friends at Le Cercle des Gourmettes was a Parisian named Louisette Bertholle. Although she was a less-impassioned cook than Simca, and had none of Julia's intellectual zeal—Paul Child called her "a charming little nincompoop"—Louisette was bright and chic and full of enthusiasm. Together the three women hatched the idea of opening a school, perhaps in Louisette's kitchen, where they could teach cooking to Americans. But before they could do much more than think about the possibility, a couple of Julia's friends from California turned up in Paris and asked Julia if she could give them cooking lessons. In January 1952, Julia, Simca, and Louisette hastily opened their school, using Julia's kitchen because Louisette's was being renovated. "A small informal cooking class, with emphasis on the 'cook hostess' angle, is 'L'Ecole des Trois Gourmandes,' which is open for five pupils," ran a notice in the embassy's in-house newsletter. "The meetings are Tuesdays and Wednesdays from 10:00 a.m. through lunch, in the home of Mrs. Paul Child. The fee is 2,000 francs including lunch, which is prepared and served by the group. There are three experienced instructors, who teach basic recipes, bourgeoise or haute cuisine." The three instructors were not quite ready for showtime, Julia admitted to her family, but they were learning as fast as they could. She knew that her life's work had begun.

These classes became the template for all the teaching that followed, both on television and in books. The atmosphere was "homey and fun and informal," and every time a student made a mistake, Julia launched a discussion of what had gone wrong and how to avoid it. After the school had been in operation for a few months, Julia typed out for herself a "*petit discours*"—a little speech she could give at the opening of each two-day course. Though it's unlikely that she used these exact words when she addressed the pupils, it's clear that her principles had settled into place. "Our aim is to teach you how to cook," she started out. "We are prepared to show the basic methods of French cooking, which, when you have mastered them, should enable you to follow a recipe, or invent any 'little dish' that you want. We feel that when one has learned to use one's tools quickly and efficiently one can then provide one's own short-cuts. . . . The recipes we give you are basic recipes, with practically no frills. We want them to be as clear and complete as possible. And we want you to feel, after we have done something in class, that you really have understood all about doing it." Everything was here—the emphasis on fundamentals, the commitment to precision and clarity, and the ultimate goal of instilling self-confidence in the cook. Later on, Paul designed an insignia for the school: a "3" in a circle, with "Ecole des Gourmandes" in flowing script around it. Julia wore it as a badge for decades, and it was always pinned to her blouse when she appeared as the "French Chef."

For each two-hour class, Julia typed up and distributed all the recipes they would be working on; and she also prepared a detailed teaching plan so that each instructor—"Prof. Julia," "Prof. Simca," and "Prof. Louisette"—would know exactly what she was supposed to do, and when. On March 12, 1952, for instance, the lesson for the day included *blanquette de veau,* or veal stew; risotto and plain rice; *salade mimosa;* and two tarts, banana and fruit. First came the introductory remarks by "Prof. Julia." Then work on the *blanquette* began, with Prof. Julia teaching the meat, the shallots, and the parsley, and Prof. Simca working with the onions and mushrooms. (Prof. Louisette, who was caught in a terrible marriage and was trying to get out, did less teaching than the others in the early years of the school.) "During this time, Prof. Julia cleans up, puts rice water to boil," the schedule read. Prof. Simca took charge of the *crème pâtissière,* or pastry cream; Prof. Julia, the salad and the *velouté* sauce for the veal; and Prof. Simca the final liaison of cream and egg yolks. (Apparently the lesson went very well—Julia scribbled "good menu" on the sheet.) On the day the plan featured quiche lorraine, puff pastry, steak *à la bordelaise,* and the meringue layer cake known as a *dacquoise,* Julia admitted the menu had been "too rich";

and on another occasion she decided the recipes were just too complicated for beginners. No matter what problems may have plagued the cooking, however, every class ended with a triumphant lunch for the teachers, the students, and their guests, typically a husband or two. When school was not in session, Julia and Simca got together in the kitchen to put their teaching recipes into what Julia called "scientific workability." They had to be "painfully exact," she told her family—"viz: exactly how much gelatine in exactly how much liquid per exactly how much mayonnaise so you can make pretty curlicues on a fish." At her request, the family sent over a set of measuring cups and spoons, which were unknown in France.

Julia also gave solo lessons, the first to a French woman who wanted to learn puff pastry. Though Julia had made it dozens of times and thought she understood it, she gave herself a practice session before the class and analyzed every step of the teaching to make sure it would be clear and accurate. Even so, there were two mistakes in the course of the lesson. Afterward, she decided she still lacked the "divine self-confidence" that identified a fine cook. "I want every technique to be perfect," she told the family with determination, "and if there are errors , they must be made on purpose." More and more, she could envision teaching at her own school, which she pictured in the kitchen of their Washington house.

Many of the recipes used at L'Ecole des Trois Gourmandes originated with Simca and Louisette, who had been working for years on a French cookbook for Americans. Their idea was to produce a wide-ranging collection of recipes with sections on wines, cheeses, and regional specialties, all authentically French, but written in English and published in the United States. Louisette, who was half American and had a number of friends and contacts in the United States, had taken the manuscript with her on one of her trips to New York and offered it to Sumner Putnam, head of a publishing company called Ives Washburn. Putnam was interested, but he had no experience with cookbooks and was unsure of the market. The manuscript, moreover, was in poor shape. Simca and Louisette had written it in French, and although they had come up with a rough English translation, it needed a great deal of work. Putnam hired a translator and cookbook author, Helmut Ripperger, for the job and asked him to produce a kind of teaser for the book—a little recipe collection drawn from the manuscript and titled "What's Cooking in France." Simca and Louisette had signed a contract for the teaser but never saw "What's Cooking" before it was published. It turned out to be an embarrassment, full of errors, and the women were distraught. In August 1952, they turned to Julia for help. The original manuscript had to be put into decent English before anything else could happen with the book—Would she take a look? Julia sat down with the sauce chapter and started to read with a pen in her hand. She had been teaching from some of these recipes, reworking them whenever necessary; and she also had done a good deal of research and recipe writing for herself. Now she tried to take the point of view of an American homemaker opening a new cookbook. She went into the kitchen and tested a few, exactly as they were written, and found them unusable. Some recipes were too abbreviated, others ran on forever with needless complications, and the instructions were infuriatingly vague. She couldn't see anything worth saving and said exactly that to Simca and Louisette. By the end of November, the three women had worked up an entirely new plan for the book, and Julia wrote to Putnam to explain what they wanted to do.

They would produce a teaching manual, she told Putnam, not just a recipe collection, and they would build it around fundamental themes and their variations. It would be written in what Julia called "the informal human approach"—a natural speaking voice, as opposed to the cloying tones of so many food writers whenever the subject was France. There were other French cookbooks for Americans, she conceded, but none was logical; none emphasized what Julia called "the 'whys,' the pitfalls, the remedies, the keeping, the serving"; none was specifically dedicated to rescuing the hapless and setting them on the right path. The new book would do all this while spanning the entire territory of basic and elaborate French cooking. She told Putnam to expect the revised chapter on sauces very shortly, and said the rest of the manuscript might take another six months.

Julia quickly became the de facto head of the project.

The whole idea thrilled her: she would be a professional writer and culinary authority, Prof. Julia on a larger stage. The more she identified with this new public persona, the more eager she was to get a lawyer involved with the project in order to put it on a businesslike basis and help them deal with Ives Washburn. She had heard a lot of horror stories about writers' experiences with their publishers. "I've gathered it's a cut-throat game and that if you don't get a lawyer or agent on your side who knows all the ropes, you can get your face peeled and all your efforts bring in the mazuma only for the publisher," she explained to Paul Sheeline, a lawyer she trusted because he was a nephew of Paul's.

Julia didn't write this book or any other primarily for the money, but she hated to feel she was being cheated or exploited, and from the beginning of her career, she made a point of being involved in the finances. She was already dubious about Ives Washburn because of the way it had botched "What's Cooking in France," and since Simca and Louisette had no formal contract with the company, she decided they should jump ship and look for a better publisher. Their book was going to be a definitive contribution to French cookery, and she was adamant that the stature and dignity of the enterprise be taken seriously. For Julia, it was the same as being taken seriously herself. "Now I've started in writing, I intend to keep at it for years and years," she told Sheeline. "So I think it wise to start out on a very firm footing." Sheeline was no specialist in cookbooks, but he did know how hard it was for first-time authors to get published, and he tried to get Julia to put the situation in perspective. "Almost any deal that can be made by a budding writer with a publisher is a good one," he counseled, and said Julia should consider herself lucky to have any publisher at all interested in her work, even Ives Washburn. This sort of thinking infuriated her. "I quite appreciate the fact that unknown authors are unknown authors," she retorted. "However, we have a good product to sell, which I think will sell itself, and I see no reason to crawl about on our stomach. This is no amateur affair written by some little women who just love to cook, but a professional job written by professionals; and, I would say without modesty, even a 'major work' on the principles of French Cooking. I therefore have no intention of wasting it on a no-account firm."

At the time Julia was taking this magisterial stand, the three authors had little in hand except the revised chapter on sauces and some early work on poultry. Even a "no-account" firm wouldn't have signed up a trio of unknown women on the basis of their hollandaise recipe. What they needed was somebody knowledgeable about cookbook publishing who would fall in love with the project and steer this cumbersome, audacious dream toward the real world; and in the spring of 1952, that very person came into Julia's life. Avis DeVoto was a writer, editor, and literary agent who lived in Cambridge, Massachusetts, with her husband, Bernard DeVoto, a political journalist and historian with a regular column in *Harper's* called "The Easy Chair." One of his columns caught Julia's attention because he was complaining about American knives. Why were they so inadequate? he demanded. Stainless steel knives were beautiful but useless; they wouldn't hold an edge. Julia agreed wholeheartedly and went out and bought a good French knife, which she mailed to him. Avis, a sophisticated cook who had suggested the column in the first place, was delighted. She wrote a thank-you letter, Julia wrote back, and the two of them fell into an absorbing correspondence.

Since moving to Paris and discovering the passion that would shape her future, Julia had been growing into herself, experiencing more and more of the sense of rightness that had started to emerge back in the OSS. It was in the course of this evolution that Avis became her chief confidante, a wonderfully witty and perceptive recipient for all Julia's musings, rants, and bouts of philosophy. Julia would type on and on, astonishing herself by how much she had to say to this faraway friend whom she'd never met in person. Sometimes she would sit under the hair dryer at the beauty parlor with paper and pen, scribbling away until, as she said, she was "baked to a turn." Avis couldn't stop talking either: the two of them scrambled from food to cookbook matters to reports on daily life to complaints and wishes and self-scrutiny, all the while pressing each other for opinions on everything from shallots to sex. Both their husbands, they discovered, liked "barbarian" food—roasts, steaks, lots of spices, lots of garlic. "I think that is very American male," Julia decided. Avis thought the Kinsey reports were a big bore; Julia was riveted by them. ("Heaven knows, I am no authority on sex, but I think it is a fine institution which should be enjoyed by all to the fullest extent.") Avis loved England, Julia much preferred France; Avis liked martinis, Julia begged her to try a good red wine. Early on, the two friends exchanged photographs. "That is a wonderfully worldly expression you have on," Julia remarked admiringly. "It is the face I always try to wear when I am in New York, with no success." She also added relevant physical details:

> *Paul,* 5'11", weight 175, very muscley. He has done lots of woodchopping, etc., and is a 3rd-degree black-belt Judo man (which is a remarkable thing).
>
> *Julia,* 6 ft. plus, weight 150 to 160. Bosom not as copious as she would wish, but has noticed that Botticelli bosoms are not big either. Legs OK, according to husband. Freckles.

And she sent interior snapshots as well. Paul, she said, was an intellectual, always ready to probe new ideas, always working on training his mind. "Me, I am not an intellectual," she admitted. "Except for La Cuisine, I find I have to push myself to build up a thirst for how the atomic bomb works, or a study of Buddhism." She attributed this problem to her childhood in a "useless and wasteful class of society." Not until she joined the OSS and was thrown in with "intellectuals and academicians" did she find the sort of people she liked. "You, however, have had years of it," she reflected. Across the ocean, in a house near Harvard Square, Avis was living one of Julia's imagined lives, just as Simca in her French kitchen was living another.

But for the first seven years of their friendship, Julia and Avis talked more than anything else about the book. As soon as the sauces chapter was fully revised, Julia sent it to Avis asking for an honest opinion as well as any advice about publishing. Avis turned every page with mounting admiration. This was a revelatory approach to French cooking: the infrastructure of culinary methods was as pertinent as the recipes, and the recipes were the most precise and logical she had ever seen. A good American cook would be able to follow them, not necessarily with ease, but at least with a sense of confidence that the authors were never going to leave her in the lurch. And, as she found in the kitchen, the recipes worked. The ingredients came together just as the instructions said they would, and the sauces tasted French. She quickly wrote back to Julia: she must keep right on working; she must not sign with Ives Washburn; Avis was going to send the chapter to a friend at Houghton Mifflin, which was a major publishing company based in Boston, and the book would be handled the way it deserved.

Julia was overjoyed—"I would say *excited*, which is my real reaction, but am learning not to use that word because of its more carnal implications in French!" The chapter went to Dorothy de Santillana, managing editor at Houghton Mifflin, who was, Avis reported, "tickled pink" with the depth and expertise of what she saw. A contract followed, along with an impressive advance of $750. "HOORAY," typed Julia. "The book will be dedicated to you, my dear, and to La Belle France." Avis refused the dedication but agreed to be the chief editorial go-between. It had all happened in less than six weeks. Julia tried to be realistic about what lay ahead: she thought it would be a year, at least, before she and her two coauthors completed the manuscript. Her prediction was off by six years, but in every other respect she understood just where she stood in her life. As she said to Avis, the midwife who would see her through a long labor, "I realize with awesome seriousness that the real work is about to begin."

Chapter 3

How to Make Things Taste the Way They Should

French cooking for American cooks? It had to be an oxymoron. How could these two incompatible beasts ever be yoked together? But Julia knew it was possible, because it had happened to her. Now she envisioned a culinary America where it happened to everyone: where ordinary home cooks made perfect creamy omelets, kept a useful supply of mirepoix on hand, boned the duck themselves, and always served a welcoming little first course when friends came to dinner. Alas, most Americans would never encounter the Cordon Bleu. The homemaker who wanted to cook something French had nothing to help her but recipes; and how miserably they could fail a hopeful cook, Julia knew well. She had spent years floundering in the awkward gap between the cookbook and the cook, until good teaching set her free. The book she would deliver to Houghton Mifflin must be just that teacher. There was no precedent for such a thing: a guide to authentic French cooking that sat on the kitchen counter calmly issuing instructions and advice in English on what to do, and what problems to expect, and how to fix them. Over the next seven years, as she worked on the manuscript, she circled round and round the core message she wanted to convey, phrasing it this way and that in an effort to pin down a heretical idea that kept prodding at her. What she wanted to tell everyone was this: French food is uniquely French, but a sure and precise route to it can be mapped in any language.

Julia's approach to the cookbook project was simple and vast: she would look at every dish in the traditional home repertoire from every perspective she could think of, testing and revising until she came up with a recipe that was absolutely foolproof and irreproachably true to its origins. When Avis asked her once why the book was taking so long, Julia described a typical day's work, in this instance a day devoted to cabbage soups. She had climbed upstairs to the kitchen with an armful of recipes: Simca's cabbage soup, numerous other cabbage soups that Julia had gathered from authoritative French cookbooks, and several regional variations. After studying all of them, she decided to try three, following two of them exactly as written and adapting the third for a pressure cooker. Obviously pressure cookers were not traditional, and Julia disliked them on aesthetic grounds ("Stinking, nasty bloody pressure cookers, I hate them!"), but if they could be made to produce good soups, she wanted to know about it. This particular experiment was a flop; the soup had an overprocessed flavor she had come to associate with pressure cookers. Nonetheless, she would keep trying: "Maybe I don't use it right, but I *will* persist with an open if distasteful mind."

The conventionally made soups were better, but she was still a long way from having a usable recipe. "I feel 1) there has got to be a good stock of veg. and ham before the cabbage is put in, and that that is one of the 'secrets' 2) that the cabbage must not be cooked too long." Maybe the cabbage would behave better if it were blanched first. Or maybe a different variety of cabbage would be an improvement. "So, all these questions of how and why and what's the point of it, have to be ironed out," she concluded. "Otherwise, you get just an ordinary recipe, and that's not the point of the book."

One of the reference books she kept close at hand was *La Bonne Cuisine de Madame E. Saint-Ange*, first published in 1927 and a bible in millions of French households. Julia often said it was her favorite French cookbook, and she would have been very pleased to see the English translation that finally appeared in 2005. Little is known about Madame Saint-Ange, except that her remarkable expertise ranged from restaurant haute cuisine to economical family cookery; but whenever Julia opened this volume, she found a mission and a sensibility exactly like her own. The recipes didn't just parade through the book: Madame Saint-Ange was teaching fundamental techniques as well as some thirteen hundred specific dishes, and she made constant reference to the history of French culinary practice and style as she moved from soups to meats to vegetables to desserts with the wisdom of a professional. Yet she could look at any given recipe as if she were an everyday home cook with a penchant for disaster. Her discussion of scrambled eggs started with a detailed scrutiny of the proper pan, then considered several methods of beating the eggs and compared the merits of a whisk versus a wooden spoon, then specified the exact shape of the wooden spoon if that was the utensil chosen, and finally proceeded carefully through the cooking, with instructions on how to avoid crises and how to undertake rescues as necessary. She did all this in a voice so calm and cheerful that whatever she was describing sounded perfectly within the reach of any attentive cook. Julia's precise debt to Madame Saint-Ange is hard to quantify—the Frenchwoman's recipes stand behind Julia's along with many other sources of inspiration—but if Madame Saint-Ange had lived long enough to translate, modernize, and fully Americanize her great work, she might well have come up with *Mastering the Art of French Cooking.*

As soon as Julia started to focus on the manuscript in her sharply analytical fashion, she ran into a problem that would keep her in a simmering rage for years. In culinary France, women like Julia—ambitious, intellectual, and irreverent—were not supposed to exist. Madame Saint-Ange was a rare exception to the rule. Women's place in French cuisine was an honored but quite specific one: it was back home in the provinces, where untutored *mamans* of legendary talent turned out the magnificent meals their sons remembered forever. This was not Julia's view of her role. To make matters worse, she was an American; and everyone in France knew for a fact that Americans were pathetic dullards who subsisted on canned food and floppy bread and had never heard of garlic. Dearly though she loved the French, this curtain of smugness, condescension, and superiority that dropped into place whenever the conversation turned to food drove her wild. "There is just an enormous amount of dogmatism to be gotten through in this country," she complained to Avis. "Cooking being a major art, there are all sorts of men's gastronomical societies, and books, and great names, and 'The real ways' of doing things, many of which have become sacred cows." Julia was painfully aware of how much she still had to learn, and she wasn't about to put one word into print that hadn't been backed up with research and testing. Yet this profound respect for accuracy seemed to count for nothing, compared with the airy certainties of Frenchmen whose culinary wisdom was based in sentiment, not science. "At the party was a dogmatic meatball who considers himself a gourmet but is just a big bag of wind," she reported indignantly to Avis. "They were talking about Beurre Blanc, and how it was a mystery, and only a few people could do it, and how it could only be made with white shallots from Lorraine over a *wood fire*. Phoo. But that is so damned typical, making a damned mystery out of perfectly simple things just to puff themselves up. I didn't say anything as, being a foreigner, I don't know anything anyway."

Practical down to her toes, Julia did not believe that mysteries were in any way related to good cooking. The idea that wondrous and ineffable traditions were granted pride of place among French gastronomes, while her own rigorous testing was seen as the pleasant little pastime of an embassy wife, infuriated her. "Discuss—Dogmatism," she scribbled on the Trois Gourmandes class schedule one day. She wanted the pupils to be aware that whenever they heard a French food lover talking about the "real" bouillabaisse, or the "real" cassoulet, they should be wary: different households made different bouillabaisses, and they were all "real." To Julia, traditional French cooking was resilient, a living thing that flowed this way and that across time and through one kitchen after another. But if that was the case, if authenticity wandered from this household to that, what held the tradition together? What made French cooking French?

When it became apparent that this was how Julia was thinking about the project, and that work on the cookbook was going to be finicky, tedious, and research-driven, Louisette drifted away. Years later, she would produce cookbooks of her own, but she just didn't think about the kitchen the way Simca and Julia did. From time to time she sent along a few ideas, but her participation was minimal. Julia wasn't surprised. "I think the book is out of her depth," she told Avis. "She is the charming 'little woman' with a talent and a taste for cooking, but a most disorganized and ultra feminine mind." Still, the book had been Louisette's idea in the first place; she was a good friend, and her home life was falling apart. Simca and Julia didn't have the heart to turn their backs on her. Louisette's name remained as coauthor, but she was allotted a smaller percentage of the royalties.

So the working team became Simca and Julia, two loving colleagues who fought their way through every recipe in the book. Fundamentally, they were incompatible—Simca wielded her intuition, Julia her intellect—which made for an exhausting collaboration but did produce a manuscript true to both of them. Avis, who watched them cooking together in Julia's kitchen in Provence one winter, said afterward that Simca was too excitable to win most of their arguments: she was constantly waving knives in the air, clashing pans around, and speaking floods of high-speed French. Julia used similar tactics but kept her wits about her and wore down her opponent by sheer tenacity. Paul thought that the reason they never actually tore each other's hair out was that for all their differences, "both have their eyes on the target rather than on themselves."

The division of labor was clear from the start: Simca's job was to be French, and Julia's was to be American. Simca had no trouble with this assignment: her recipes and all her experience in the kitchen flowed from the culture in which she grew up. She had French cooking, as Avis put it, "in her blood and bones." Many of her recipes were original, but they were all outcroppings from the culinary tradition she had inherited and tended with care. To stand back and scrutinize the tradition objectively did not come easily to her: it was like trying to diagram the flavor of apples.

Julia, by contrast, was an American by temperament as well as birth who heartily believed in the scientific approach. To her, French culinary tradition was a frontier, not a religion, and the evidence of things unseen was no evidence at all. Although her favorite cookbook from home was *Joy of Cooking*, Julia had in her more than a touch of Fannie Farmer—the dedicated, charismatic cooking teacher who introduced level measurements in the late nineteenth century because her students wanted to know what "a pinch" of salt was, and how much flour was meant by "a handful." Like Miss Farmer, who was a leader in the moral and culinary reform movement known as scientific cookery, Julia saw a higher realm waiting for those who mastered the skills of the kitchen; and she shared Miss Farmer's certainty that painstaking methods and precise instructions had the power to transform both the cooking and the cook. To be sure, Julia's vision of a higher realm was one rampant with pleasure, conviviality, and the free play of the senses. This was hardly what the pious founders of scientific cookery had in mind for their students and followers, whose lessons sometimes culminated in an all-white dinner evoking a temple of purity. But Julia believed as they did that good cooking was pragmatic cooking, a matter of forming the right habits and using them daily—a discipline, not a burst of inspiration. One day she took a piece of notepaper and wrote "A good cook" at the top of it. Then she jotted down a definition: "is consistently good—not just a little flair here & there—She can turn out a good meal either simple or complicated, can adapt herself to conditions, and has enough exp. to change a failure into a success. If the fish doesn't moose [mousse]—it becomes a soup. Matter of practice & passion." Practice and passion: Julia put them together and kept them there in all her teaching and writing, twin imperatives that were useless when separated.

During the years that she and Simca were working on the book, they rarely inhabited the same kitchen. Paul was posted to Marseille in 1954, then to Bonn, then back home to Washington, and finally to Oslo before retiring in 1961. Although the two women were able to visit each other occasionally for marathon cooking sessions, most of their discussions and fights were carried on by letter. Recipes, notes, suggestions, additions, revisions, and corrections flew back and forth, sometimes in quantities that would have merited a doctoral degree in any other discipline. When Julia launched an assault on cassoulet—a rich and hefty assortment of beans, meats, and sausages that could take up to three days to prepare—she first rounded up twenty-eight recipes, all authentic from reputable sources, many of them contradictory. She and Simca winnowed them down, combining and refining and rewriting until they reached a single, triumphant version, all the while carrying on a blazing argument about preserved goose. Few American households were likely to have access to preserved goose, but Simca insisted it was essential: without it, they couldn't call the dish cassoulet. Mutton stew, perhaps. But not cassoulet. Julia pounded her with source after source that omitted preserved goose. At length Julia won, though the two families ate many more cassoulets than anyone wished before a truce was declared.

Other recipes were simpler, but everything required numerous tweaks and tinkerings before both women were satisfied. Working on spinach, Julia picked up an idea from a book and dashed off a note in the scramble of French and English with which she always wrote to Simca. "Suggestion which comes from A. Suzanne, a contemporary of Escoffier, which is to put une pointe d'ail in les epinards, especially 'au jus,' and even à la crème. So small it is hardly noticeable, it does a certain amount of relevement which is very agreeable. Please try." Every nuance counted; every minor shift in method had to be recorded. "I want every detail from you that you can think of," Julia begged. "Whether or not I use the detail is of no matter, I want it anyway. People must say of this book, A MARVELOUS BOOK. I've never been able to make cake before, but now I can."

This imagined reader, the desperate homemaker who couldn't cook until the right book fell into her hands, had a permanent place in Julia's consciousness and directly inspired the immense amount of detail that characterized her recipes. Like a ghost from Julia's own past, she trailed Julia from kitchen to desk and back again, forever trying to figure out whether the roast was done, why the chops were steaming in the pan instead of browning properly, what made the cream puffs soggy, and exactly how thick the beef slices should be: a quarter inch? an eighth of an inch? Julia often called her "the young bride." Simca, of course, had no such creature haunting her—she had been a young bride who cooked splendidly from the first day—and Julia had to plead with her to measure and test with scientific rigor. Take nothing for granted, she counseled Simca over and over. Don't ever make a statement of fact until it has been tested so many times we "absolutely know" it is true. She sent Simca a meat thermometer and measuring cups, and issued constant bulletins on her own experiments. "I have just poached two more eggs," she reported from deep within the egg chapter. "Well, the eggs weighed 60 grams or two ounces, and they do, effectivement, need 4 minutes. I also found, measuring everything again, that there should be but 1½ to 2 inches water, and the pan should be but 8 inches in diameter. Thank heaven I did it again to catch these two awful errors." Simca had a hard time keeping up with this degree of microscopic fussing, and as she moved from recipe to recipe, she kept forgetting to use the methods they had worked out so exhaustively.

Simca was an extraordinary cook, and Julia knew it, but the recipes Simca contributed from her own repertoire were far too personal to go into the book without extensive testing and revision. Not only did they need to be made scientifically precise, but Julia wanted to be sure they represented the mainstream of French tradition. What horrified Julia about many French cookbooks, especially the ones written by Americans, was that the authors seemed to feel they were free to rewrite standard recipes in any fashion they chose, and then present the result as completely classic. She was frantic with worry that the recipes she received from Simca had been Simca-fied, made delicious in Simca's hands but allowed to wander significantly off course. "It is not, my dear, that I do not have confidence in you!" she insisted in the course of a quarrel about clafoutis. "I think we are both interested, in this book, in making sure it is La Veritable Cuisine Française, and not just La Cuisine Simca/Julia." The book would have to depart from tradition at times, for instance when certain ingredients weren't available in America, but Julia was adamant that whenever she and Simca altered a template, they had to say so up front. Once, when they were working together in Marseille on *sauce à la rouille*, Simca casually referred to the recipe they had developed as "Rouille Julia"—idiosyncratic, that is, and not traditional. Julia was aghast. "That is a SHOCKING remark coming from you," she wrote after the visit. "It means that you have allowed me to perpetrate a little 'popote Julia' into a book on French cooking." Simca's role, Julia reminded her, was to protect the authenticity of the recipes, even and especially from Julia herself. The most crucial piece of equipment they had was Simca's taste memory.

Simca would have been happy to rely on her own palate for the book she and Louisette had originally planned, but this book had far loftier aspirations, and they made her nervous. She and Julia were only a couple of home cooks, and women at that. How dare they contradict, in print, the old masters and professional chefs who constituted the priestly class in French cooking? The sight of the recipes she and Julia had worked so hard on, all typed up and ready for the publisher, filled her with anxiety. Often she demanded they go back and make changes in a recipe completed long ago, just because she'd come across a chef who had a different method—surely he knew better than the two of them. This stubborn diffidence made Julia impatient. "I consider ourselves just as much AUTHORITIES as anyone else," she railed. What did the sages have that she and Simca lacked? The two women had training and experience, they consulted the sources, they did a vast amount of cooking, tasting, and testing. But the confidence Julia sported so comfortably was foreign to Simca. Though she could fight fiercely, she had a streak of what Julia called "*obéissance*," or "obedience"—an instinct Julia thought was typical of Frenchwomen who tended to defer to men far too readily. A year and a half into their collaboration, Julia sent Simca—"Ma plusque chère Colleague"—three rules to live by:

> Stand up for *your* opinions as an equal partner in this enterprise.
>
> Keep the book French.
>
> Follow the scientific method, respecting your *own* careful findings, after having studied the findings and

> recommendations of other authorities. Work with exact measurements, temperatures, etc. And, once having established a method, stick to it religiously unless you find it is not satisfactory.

(Then she tossed in a postscript: "Please, also, learn to cut professionally with a knife. Who knows, we may end up on television, and you must establish professional techniques.")

For Julia, the moral barometer for this project was not fidelity to the old masters but fidelity to the food. Those first months in France, when she spent day after day plunging into flavors of an intensity she had never known before, had left a permanent stain on her senses. To have lived so long without this! Now she was determined to re-create that food by writing recipes so precise, so perfect, that each was a miniature version of the discovery that had transformed her. She was on a quest for *le gout français*—the very flavor of Frenchness. Like any flavor, this one was hard to describe in words, but instantly recognizable on the palate. Julia never doubted for a moment that the quintessential taste of France was portable, that it could be realized by any cook, anywhere, with the right instructions. She and Simca were going to capture that taste, press it like a butterfly onto every page of their book. And unlike Simca, she knew she would have no qualms about claiming victory. This was cooking, not alchemy; the only secrets were spread out on the kitchen counter for all to see: butter and eggs and string beans, whisks and saucepans and measuring spoons. Nothing mysterious, nothing unquantifiable. "If one is using French methods and French ingredients or as near an equivalent as can be found, one achieves GOUT FRANÇAIS," she said flatly.

The moment she used the term *French ingredients*, of course, she had to qualify it. Many of the ingredients that Americans would have to use would be "as near an equivalent as can be found," and some of them wouldn't be all that near. But Julia was never the sort of gastronome who thought great cooking began and ended with perfect ingredients; she was far too pragmatic for that. It's not that she was immune to their splendor: like every other American eating in Paris for the first time, she had been dazzled by the startlingly bright flavors of the fresh fruits and vegetables. "Strawberries, for instance, are dreamberries," she wrote to Avis. "Beans are so deliciously beany. They haven't yet gotten on to the system of growing a tough variety that will keep well in the markets." Yet she quite forgot to include in the manuscript any mention of how important it was to use the best possible ingredients; and when she remembered, about a year before the book was published, she merely shrugged. Other errors in the manuscript—or worse, the index—dismayed her terribly, but not this one. It was far more important that the book fend off the popular assumption that every food item in France was superior to its American counterpart. Too many tourists came to

Paris, swooned over the food, and went home convinced that meals so glorious must spring from wondrous ingredients unique to France. Not true, Julia insisted. Spinach was spinach, and even if it wasn't, good cooking would make up for the difference.

Julia was so obsessively open-minded on the subject of American ingredients that she wouldn't even exclude canned and frozen products, at least not without giving them a chance to prove themselves. French gastronomes thought packaged foods were barbaric, and sophisticated Americans were embarrassed by them, but Julia wanted her recipes to be within reach of every home cook who could summon the ambition to try them. If a box of frozen peas, or a can of bouillon, honestly merited a place in a traditional French recipe, the book should say so. There was nothing to be gained by snobbery. She shopped for such products at the embassy commissary and devoted long testing sessions to them, generally with grim results. "I have just served my poor husband the most miserable lunch of frozen haddock Dugléré, frozen 'fresh' string beans and 'minute' rice," she wrote to Avis after an early effort in 1953. "It is just no fun to eat that stuff, no matter how many French touches and methods you put to it. It ain't French, it ain't good, and the hell with it."

That afternoon, Julia went out for a restorative walk along one of her favorite streets, rue de Seine, and came home in a better mood. But she wasn't going to quit: she would continue experimenting even though by their very nature these products threw a wet blanket over the kitchen. Where was the tactile pleasure of handling food, where were the smells, and where oh where were the flavors? "Got a frozen roasting chicken the other day," she reported to Avis. "It was mushy, a bit chewy, and had very little taste. It had, also, a slightly rancid-fat overtone." She tried warming half of it in a coq au vin sauce, which lent a little flavor but not enough to salvage the product or win it a mention in the book. "If things aint good, they aint; we are not in the frozen food lobby." To her astonishment, instant potatoes turned out to be pretty good, though requiring quite a bit of butter, cream, and cheese. Uncle Ben's Converted Brand Rice became such a favorite she took to calling it "*l'Oncle Ben's,*" and she was so delighted with instant piecrust mix that she sent a box to Simca and told her she must try it. Simca was not impressed: she disliked the taste of vegetable shortening in place of butter. Julia admitted the flavor wasn't really French. "However, they certainly are easy and certainly perfectly good. And certainly better for that average housewife, French or US, who would otherwise make a horrid crust," she argued.

In a way, she was arguing with herself more than with Simca. At the time she tried piecrust mix, she was living in Washington, D.C., and taking careful note of how Americans behaved in the kitchen. So many of them lacked basic skills or were reluctant to take the time to do things well. Was the point of the book to get better-tasting food on the American table, by any means necessary? Or was the purpose to make real changes, to move wonderful food to the center of American life? One day she was working on glacéed carrots and onions and decided to save time by using canned onions. The result was so awful she shot off a letter to Simca. "I DO NOT LIKE CANNED ONIONS AT ALL," she announced. "I suggest that we say: WE DO NOT LIKE CANNED ONIONS. Period." The incessant American preoccupation with saving time was getting on her nerves. "I think we cannot compromise on the techniques of making things taste the way they should taste even if some refusals to take the easy way result in some time-consuming operations," she decided. "Our book is on how to make things taste the way they should." In the end, pie-crust mixes did not get into the pastry chapter.

But in other respects, the two years in Washington were revelatory. Supermarkets she found to be a splendid innovation: she loved pushing her cart through the aisles and getting a good view and feel of everything on display. Unlike a charming little French market, where the shopkeeper picked out the items for each customer, these huge, impersonal stores left her free to select exactly the mushrooms she wanted, the very bunch of parsley that looked best to her. "It is so heavenly to go to the asparagus counter and pick out each individual spear yourself, or each single string bean," she exclaimed to Simca. "The asparagus is perfectly delicious! This is the season where they come by rapid transit from California, and are great fat green spears, sweet, tender and perfect." Back in France she had been sure that if produce had to be shipped cross-country, there was no hope for flavor, but now she was eating fine springtime asparagus and doing so with delight.

At the same time, however, disappointments were piling up. Her quest for decent American chicken—whole or in parts, fresh or frozen, supermarket or butcher shop—went on for years. Butter, the most beloved ingredient in her kitchen, was tasteless compared with its French counterpart; and thick, matured cream with the nutty flavor of French cream was nowhere to be found. Shallots were expensive and rarely available; nobody would be able to buy a calf's foot or a pig's caul; the veal was inferior to French, and the only fresh herb in sight was parsley. What's more, Americans had the irritating habit of not drinking wine. That was regrettable in itself, but if they didn't drink wine regularly, they weren't going to have it on hand for cooking, and wine was essential for flavor. Conceivably they might buy a bottle of inexpensive California red just for cooking, but the inexpensive California whites were dreadful, in Julia's estimation. Avis wondered whether vermouth might be a substitute, since people tended to have it around for cocktails. Julia rejected the idea at first, because the "strong and herbal taste" would throw off the flavor of sauces. But after living in Washington for a while, she relented. "People just do not have bottles of white wine all the time to use in cooking," she explained to Simca. "If they bought one for a bit of cooking, they wouldn't know what to do with the rest of it. Therefore I think we must always specify the choice of White Vermouth, as everybody has that; and it will keep after having been opened." She experimented with proportions and found that if she used vermouth more sparingly than wine in delicate sauces, the flavor was satisfactory.

Clearly, there could be nothing rigid or pristine about the concept of ingredients in this book. That didn't bother Julia at all. On the contrary, she thought it was in the very nature of ingredients to be pliable, to serve the cook no matter where the cook was heading. She had always hated that brand of wisdom about bouillabaisse that insisted the only proper versions came from grizzled French fishermen in certain coastal towns. She had had a terrible bouillabaisse in the coastal town of Le Lavandou—"very rough, and flavored with nothing but saffron"—and decided she was probably a better cook than most grizzled fishermen. She proceeded to make bouillabaisse everywhere she lived, from Maine to Norway, using the likeliest fresh fish available, and found the results not only delicious but impeccably French. A slew of freshly caught pollack was the basis for her Maine bouillabaisse: with potatoes, fennel, and saffron, she reported to Simca, "It was very good, and had the correct taste . . . the necessary flavor was there." What made a dish French wasn't the raw materials, it was what happened to them in the hands of the cook.

Strawberries were dreamberries—she ate them with rapture every summer she found herself in France—but the key that unlocked French cooking for Julia was technique.

Her lessons with Chef Bugnard had turned her toward a radiant future. In the logic and transparency of culinary method, each step a meaningful contribution to the complex beauty of the result, Julia had found her lifelong faith. She was a believer, not in the dogma set down by the sages, but in the notion of French cooking as a great master plan—fundamental procedures that could be applied to all the cuisines of the world. Learning to cook, moreover, had unleashed her imagination, her powers of analysis, her scholarly skills, and her addiction to hard work. Simple dishes, well prepared, would always win her respect; but Julia liked cooking best when it was akin to mountain climbing, not a stroll in the park. She went into the kitchen because that was the place where her mind was engaged most happily and energetically. Years later, when her friend Anne Willan was planning the curriculum for La Varenne, the Paris cooking school, Julia urged her to establish a place early in the schedule for "difficult or advanced items, like puff pastry." The size and scope of the demand constituted, to Julia, the very essence of her chosen work. As she put it to Willan, "The sooner one gets to pastry, the more of a cook one begins to feel." By contrast, the whole question of ingredients was negotiable. Canned and frozen foods, vermouth instead of wine—these couldn't erode or undermine the Frenchness of the cooking. But when a French cookbook devoted to shortcut recipes appeared—*Cuisine d'Urgence,* or "Hurry-up Cooking"—Julia read doom on every page. If technique was lost, if careful methods gave way to speed for its own sake, the end was nigh. "I find the sauce-making methods horrifying, and also disturbing, and hope that too many people will not take to it," she wrote to Simca. "It will be the death of La Cuisine Fcse."

Yet even on the subject of technique, she was willing to consider modern innovations if they achieved the right results. At the Cordon Bleu she had learned to whip egg whites with a balloon whisk, to beat butter by hand, to keep constant watch over the egg yolks while making hollandaise to be sure they were thickening properly and absorbing the right amount of butter, and to employ hours of pounding and sieving and beating to make quenelles. Now she bought a blender and an electric mixer and started to experiment. "This whole field is wide open, that of using the electric aids for a lot of fancy French stuff, and we'll be presenting something entirely new," she told Avis. "No sacred cows for us." She was delighted to outdo the old masters by using a mixer to beat cream into the quenelle paste, or using a blender instead of a mortar and pestle to make shellfish butter. But even when the electric aids did a good job, she was careful about how she expressed her approval. If a machine saved the cook from a truly laborious chore, she recommended it outright. But when machines became a substitute for the cook's skill, for her practiced hand and her powers of observation—when they made it possible for someone to cook as if she, too, were a machine—Julia hedged. Yes, you can make hollandaise and mayonnaise in the blender, she assured readers, and included recipes for both the traditional and machine versions. But she begged readers to become adept at making these sauces by hand so they could examine close-up what was happening to the egg yolks. Even an eight-year-old could make blender hollandaise, she added—a remark that wasn't necessarily an endorsement. Julia never believed good cooking was child's play. As she scribbled in her notes while writing the introduction to the book, "Life is hard & earnest. Most pains—most results. If know what doing—half battle is won."

Long hours in the kitchen, hard labor, page after page of instructions, unfamiliar food—Julia did wonder occasionally whether American homemakers were going to be as enthusiastic as she was about these recipes. American newspapers and magazines were constantly running stories about how modern women didn't know how to cook and refused to learn, preferring to make dinner by opening boxes and cans. Even a gourmet meal, the magazines crowed, could now be put on the table in a half hour. "The advertisers have made people feel like fools if they even wanted to take time over things," Julia wrote to Simca. "There are loads and loads and loads of books and articles on how to do things quickly, and very very very few on how to make things taste good." Americans just didn't think about cooking the way the French did. Homemakers looked at recipes and worried about how many pots and pans were going to get dirty; they liked to economize by using margarine and never dreamed it could affect the flavor of the dish; they put three or four ill-matched ingredients together and served it up as a casserole. "Casseroles," Julia groaned to Avis. "I even hate the name, as it always implies to me some god awful mess." Nor could she abide the way Americans made a fetish of nutrition. "I think one should get one's vitamins in salads, and raw fruits, and what is cooked should be absolutely delicious and to hell with the vitamins." At a luncheon meeting of the American Embassy Wives Club in Oslo, Julia was served what she described to Simca as "the most horrible meal I have ever had"—a particularly lurid example of what was going on back home. "As we sat down each guest was served a big plate on which there was a tower of pink stuff posed on a piece of lettuce. This tower turned out to be about ½ litre of frozen whipped cream mixed with mayonnaise, frozen strawberries, bananas, peaches, and grapes . . . everything as hard as a rock. And the lettuce leaf was so small one couldn't hide anything under it. The next and final course was a banana and nut cake–mix cake, an enormous piece for each guest. Cake was surrounded with a very thick tan-colored frosting, also a mix I suppose, because I can't imagine anyone making it. Ugh."

But she refused to believe that frozen fruit salad had permanently numbed the American palate. Surely, if she and Simca could make their recipes clear and foolproof, American homemakers would convert. How could they resist the food, once they had tasted the first perfectly prepared chicken breasts of their lives? The first true omelets? The first cakes made light by their own billowing egg whites, not baking powder? The greater challenge would be to persuade homemakers to undertake such lengthy recipes, given their lackadaisical approach to cooking and the tremendous bugaboo of time. One solution was to do as much as possible ahead of zero hour, and Julia had long made a specialty of this strategy. The clock ticking inexorably toward dinnertime, the sense of panic, the bevy of details frantic for her attention—all this was deeply familiar to her. Throughout her work on the book, the needs of what she called "the chef-hostess" were at the forefront of her thinking. Every recipe, she told Avis, would include directions on how to prepare as much as possible of the dish ahead of time, and how to store and reheat it without sacrificing flavor or texture. "There are so many many things which can be done that way—green veg, fish in sauce, roasts, braises, sautés in sauce—etc.," she explained. "There is no reason why one has to serve those bloody casseroles all the time."

Toward the end of 1957, while Julia was living in Washington, she decided it would be a good idea to publish a few articles in American magazines. She and Simca were in the final stages of their work, readying the manuscript for delivery to Houghton Mifflin, and a little advance publicity would certainly benefit the book. After much thought about what might appeal to Americans, she prepared an article featuring the Belgian specialty *waterzoï de poulet.* It would be timely, since the 1958 World's Fair was about to open in Brussels, and she felt the recipe would pose no special difficulties to the home cook. Because her editor, Dorothy de Santillana, was based in Boston, Julia sent the article to John Leggett, who was Houghton Mifflin's New York editor, to "peddle around." She urged him to explain to magazine food editors that although the recipe was long, it was not at all complicated—merely detailed. To her amazement, there were no takers, even though the recipe required nothing more than sweating the chicken, poaching it in wine, julienning and cooking the aromatic vegetables, and making a rather tricky sauce with egg yolks, cream, and broth. Helen McCully of *McCall's* food section took one look and said that if she showed this recipe to her editor, "she would probably faint dead away." McCully added that she herself could tell what a well-constructed recipe it was, but "to the non-cook it certainly looks like quite a chore." Julia was not discouraged. She trimmed the recipe and sent it back to Leggett along with another possibility—boned stuffed duck in a pastry crust. "This is a marvelous dish, can be served hot or cold, and makes a splendid effect," she wrote hopefully. "Most people think this is the kind of impossible thing only a chef could do, but it is quite within the range of even the modest cook if supplied with good directions such as ours." She envisioned a spread in *Life:* "Life Bones a Duck."

Leggett had no success with the articles. McCully said even the shortened version of *waterzoï* was too complicated for American housewives, and the other food editors had the same reaction. For the first time, Julia started to worry that she might be horribly out of step with the rest of the country. "I am deeply depressed, gnawed by doubts, and feel that all our work may just lay a big rotten egg," she admitted to Avis. But she hated the thought of turning the recipes into baby talk just because a lot of magazine editors didn't understand French cooking. "The completed volume will, I believe, speak for itself," she told Leggett with dignity. Simca came to Washington, and the two women scrambled to finish by deadline day, February 24, 1958.

They made the deadline, but the manuscript they delivered did not speak for itself, at least in any language Houghton Mifflin could understand. The thing was a monster: eight hundred pages, and they covered only poultry and sauces. Julia's idea was that the book would be published as a series of volumes, one every two years. The next would be eggs and vegetables, then perhaps meat, then soup and fish, and so on into the future—"up to the grave, as the subject is vast," she predicted happily. She had tried to explain this plan a few months earlier to Dorothy de Santillana, who protested that Houghton Mifflin wanted a cookbook, not an infinite series of cookbooks. The misunderstanding had never been cleared up, and now De Santillana was gazing white-faced at recipes with a quantity of detail that bordered on manic. If you want to make pressed duck, Julia informed American homemakers, you'll find it hard to locate the right sort of duck—one that was killed by suffocation in order to retain the blood that enriched the sauce—so go ahead and do as so many French restaurants now do, and add fresh pig's blood mixed with wine to the duck press. "This is not the book we contracted for," De Santillana said faintly. Julia objected, but when she was able to step back and gain a little perspective on the manuscript, she could see exactly what they had delivered to Houghton Mifflin: a huge, densely overgrown thicket of brambles, impossible to handle.

De Santillana rejected the manuscript outright, but she was still impressed by Julia and Simca, and she invited them to come up with a plan for a more salable book. She even picked up on Julia's idea of a series, but said the books would have to be very different from the volume in hand. Each one must be very simple and very compact, written to fit the time and attention constraints of the typical American cook, "who is so apt to be mother, nurse, chauffeur, and cleaner as well." Julia knew this was sensible advice, but it didn't appeal to her. She was still longing to write a big, fat treatise covering every single essential point about French cooking. Nonetheless, after conferring with Simca, she decided to give in and accept the American way of life in culinary matters, or at least to go along with the prevailing pessimistic view of it. Americans seemed intent on "speed and the elimination of work," she conceded to De Santillana. "We have therefore decided to shelve our own dream for the time being and propose to prepare you a short and snappy book directed to the somewhat sophisticated housewife-chauffeur." The book would run about three hundred pages and feature authentic French recipes as well as hints on the "pepping up" of frozen and canned products. "Everything would be of the simpler sort, but nothing humdrum," she promised. "The recipes would look short. We might even manage to insert a note of gaiety and a certain quiet chic, which would be a pleasant change."

She was proposing exactly the sort of book she despised. Yes, she would try to lift it above the inanity of most magazine treatments of French cooking—"quiet chic" might help, assuming the format could support such an innovation—but she would be addressing her least favorite people in the world, the ones who firmly resisted cooking. *Housewives.* Julia had never thought one way or another about the word, but she was growing to hate it. Editors, publishers, everyone who talked about recipes in America bowed and scraped to housewives, those ubiquitous females forever depicted as running frantically from laundry to car pool to scout troop, with no time to cook excellent meals and, it was universally assumed, no desire to learn. The task facing her now would be to win the allegience of this unappealing creature. Other cookbook authors had succeeded; maybe she and Simca could at least raise the standard. She asked Avis to send her a copy of one of Houghton Mifflin's bestselling cookbooks, *Helen Corbitt's Cookbook*, by a popular Texas food expert in charge of the restaurant at Neiman Marcus. Corbitt's recipe for coq au vin was exactly twenty-five words long, not counting the list of ingredients. "It is such a wonderful example of easy-looking recipes," Julia wrote; and her admiration was sincere, though not for the food.

But after thinking about the new book for a few weeks, she had to pull back. Canned soup sauces? Casseroles bulging with frozen vegetables? Convenience first, flavor and texture last? Julia just couldn't bring herself to write for home cooks who bore such ill will toward food that they kept their contact with it to a minimum even while they were making dinner. If she and Simca were going to publish a cookbook, it had to have cooking in it; and if that meant the housewife would be frightened off, then the book would have to reach somebody else. By the time she wrote to De Santillana to confirm the new proposal, she had come up with a working formula for a book she and Simca could produce in good faith—a book that would be realistic about American life, but never cross over to the dark side. "This is to be a collection of good French dishes of the simpler sort, directed quite frankly to those who enjoy cooking and have a feeling for food," she told her editor. Thus began the writing of the manuscript that would be titled, eventually, *Mastering the Art of French Cooking*.

The goal remained the same—to reach *le gout français* by means of clear, precise recipes and supermarket ingredients—but Escoffier and the other old masters who had been peering over Julia's shoulder as she typed were now banished. No longer was she flogging herself to be "complete and exhaustive and immortal," she told Avis.

The challenge was to cut down the number and size of the recipes and reduce the verbiage, while keeping the results pristine. "I can't get oven-roasted chicken down to less than 2 pages," she complained. "If you leave out the basting and turning, it ain't a French roast." But she did it—roast chicken ran just over two pages in the published book, complete with basting, turning, sauce making, and ahead-of-time note. The new freedom in their approach also meant they could include some of Simca's own recipes for cakes and desserts, which would turn out to be among the most popular in the book.

It took about a year and a half to produce the new version, and they sent it to De Santillana in September 1959 with a great deal of confidence. She had been reading the chapters as they were finished and after poring over the entire manuscript for four days, she wrote to say that she was stunned and thrilled. "I surely do not know of any other compendium so amazingly, startlingly accurate or so inclusive," she told Julia. The good news sent Julia, Simca, and Avis soaring, but two months later they were brought back to earth with a thud. Paul Brooks, the editor in chief of Houghton Mifflin, had consulted with the business side of the company and could see no way to publish the book without losing a massive amount of money. Julia had promised a "short, simple book directed to the housewife chauffeur," Brooks reminded her. What she had delivered was very different—a book so huge, expensive, and elaborate that it was certain to seem formidable "to the American housewife."

The housewife. There she was again. Brooks assured Julia that if she wanted to give it another try, he would be glad to look at a much-reduced version of the manuscript; but Julia had gone as far into housewife territory as she was willing to go. No pressed duck, complete with history and folklore? Fine. But she wouldn't cut back on the essentials in the roast chicken recipe. She wouldn't write for any "chauffeur den-mother" who wasn't willing to meet her halfway. Defeated, dejected, and feeling guilty about letting down Simca, Julia took herself into the kitchen and started to cook. Pastry skills—here was a whole area of French cooking she knew little about and really should study. She began with *tuiles,* those very delicate cookies that must be shaped into a curve around a rolling pin as soon as they come out of the oven. "Terribly simple batter to prepare, but in none of the French recipes have I found quite the exact explanation of what is what, so I must start out blind," she told Avis eagerly. So many pitfalls! How hot should the oven be? What was the right consistency for the batter? What would keep the cookies from breaking as they were transferred from the oven to the rolling pin? Cooking—especially exploratory cooking, in search of the perfect recipe—was always the comfort zone. Now she returned to it.

While Julia was cooking, Avis was plotting. For the last several years, she had been talking about the book with her friend William Koshland, who recently had been made an executive at Alfred A. Knopf, one of the most distinguished publishing houses in the country. Koshland was a food lover and had been following the travails of the manuscript with interest. As a New Yorker with many friends in the culinary world, he was sure that Houghton Mifflin was being shortsighted and that this was exactly the right time for a good, definitive work on French cooking. Housewives might not have the time for long, unfamiliar recipes; but there were, he believed, "real cooks and hobby cooks" everywhere who would be fascinated. People were traveling, they were taking cooking lessons, they were subscribing to *Gourmet*, and they were buying the huge tomes on high-class cooking published by the magazine—"Never before has this country been so gourmet-minded," he told Avis. Most of the soothsayers in publishing saw this trend as negligible, at least compared with all the high-speed cooking that was being promoted so adamantly in the media. But something told Koshland that this book, a genuine teaching tool, had the potential to create a market of its own. As the fortunes of the manuscript rose and fell at Houghton Mifflin, Koshland kept reminding Avis he wanted Knopf to be next in line. The moment Julia heard the bad news from Houghton Mifflin, Avis had the manuscript sent directly to Alfred Knopf himself, who—like everyone else in publishing—was a friend of hers. "Do not despair," she wrote to Julia. "We have only begun to fight."

Neither Alfred Knopf nor his wife, Blanche, who ran the company with him, had any interest in bringing out a new French cookbook. They had just published *Classic French Cooking* by Joseph Donon, a protégé of Escoffier. Surely that was enough of a nod to the emerging gourmet market. Alfred didn't even glance at the manuscript, but as a courtesy to Avis he passed it along to Koshland, who was regarded as the in-house food expert. Koshland promptly handed it to a young editor named Judith Jones, who had lived in France and was a talented cook. The two of them, along with Angus Cameron—the editor who had helped launch *Joy of Cooking* years earlier at Bobbs-Merrill—worked their way through one recipe after another and grew more excited with every dish they turned out. Jones found the manuscript to be an extraordinary achievement, the first book she had ever seen that made it possible to reproduce the flavors she had loved in France. In Julia's text, Jones could recognize not only an expert cook but a personable writer and brilliant teacher. Americans would respond to this book. But they wouldn't even see it unless the Knopfs agreed, and Koshland knew what an obstacle that was. The book would be expensive to put out, he admitted to Avis, but he told her he was ready to "ram it through the board," no matter how reluctant Alfred and Blanche might be. Julia had refused to let herself feel optimistic about Knopf, especially because of the Donon book, but when she heard this—and when she learned that several editors had actually gone to their stoves and used the recipes and loved them—she allowed the tiniest "coal of hope" to begin to glow.

Koshland won, and the book was formally accepted in May 1960 with Judith Jones at the head of the immense project. For the rest of Julia's career, Jones would be the editor who counseled, inspired, steadied, and rescued her in countless ways, not only while they worked on books together but in the course of Julia's work in television, magazines, and public life. It was Jones who came up with the title *Mastering the Art of French Cooking*—nixing "French Food at Last!," "French Kitchen Pleasure," and "Love and French Cooking," among other contestants—and it was Jones who knew that even Americans might venture on board for a long, tumultuous voyage to cassoulet or French bread if Julia was piloting the ship.

Mastering the Art of French Cooking came out with a gratifying splash in October 1961. Craig Claiborne of the *New York Times* called it "glorious," "comprehensive," "laudable," and "monumental," and New York's culinary elite swarmed to a publication party hosted by Dione Lucas, who had reigned since the 1940s as the nation's leading expert in French cooking. But there was significant competition that fall, even in the small category of definitive French cookbooks. *Gourmet* brought out a fat volume called *Gourmet's Basic French Cookbook* by Louis Diat, the chef at New York's Ritz-Carlton Hotel, whose columns in the magazine Julia had admired for years. The first American edition of the famous culinary encyclopedia *Larousse Gastronomique* also turned up, with one of Julia's classmates from Smith, Charlotte Turgeon, as coeditor. And while Claiborne's own book, *The New York Times Cookbook,* wasn't specifically French, it was certainly sophisticated enough to appeal to many of the passionate home cooks Julia had counted on to buy *Mastering.* Earlier French cookbooks, including Samuel Chamberlain's beloved *Clementine in the Kitchen* and his 619-page *Bouquet de France,* were still on people's shelves, along with Dione Lucas's two books and the first *Gourmet* cookbook, which had come out in 1950 and continued to sell nicely. There did seem to be talented, ambitious home cooks in America, but perhaps they were happy with the books they already owned. Despite rapturous reviews and an exhilarating cross-country publicity tour—which Julia and Simca organized and paid for themselves—*Mastering* sold only a modest sixteen thousand copies the first year it was out.

"The sales may not be spectacular, but I have complete confidence that word of mouth will keep this going forever," Koshland assured Julia. "Word of mouth" did not impress her too much; she'd have preferred to see some advertising. Knopf had produced a splendid-looking book but didn't seem to be doing much to push it. Most of what the public knew about *Mastering* came from media attention she and Simca had generated on their tour. "Our publishers really are about as unbusinesslike as any I have encountered," she fumed to Simca. "They remind me of the little café I used to go to after my morning courses at the Cord. Bleu. One of the boys introduced me to the proprietress saying: I've brought you a new customer. Oh, she said, I have enough customers already!"

But Koshland was right, in a sense. The sales did have a

life of their own, independent of Knopf's genteel way with promotion. The target population of enthusiastic home cooks may have been slow to get to bookstores, but to everyone's surprise there seemed to be a hidden population very willing to take a stab at elaborate French cooking. In the fall of 1962, the Book-of-the-Month Club made *Mastering* a dividend selection, expecting to distribute around twelve thousand copies. By March, sixty-five thousand books had gone out, orders were still pouring in, and *Mastering* had become the most popular dividend in the history of the club. Meanwhile, *The French Chef*, which began in 1963, was making Julia a television star. As the program reached one public television station after another, bookstore sales boomed; and in 1974, *Mastering* appeared on the *New York Times* list of the century's best-selling cookbooks, with 1.3 million copies sold. Nearly a half century after publication, the book had been revised once—to introduce the food processor, among other updates—and reprinted dozens of times. It was still selling steadily at the rate of some eighteen thousand copies a year.

Once the success of the book was established in the mid-1960s, Julia and Simca started thinking about a second volume. By this time Julia was beginning to wriggle free of what she would finally term the *straitjacket* of traditional French cooking; and Volume II reflects her willingness to take liberties she didn't allow herself earlier. On the whole, Volume II was devoted to characteristic French food, including charcuterie and pastries, as well as a nineteen-page recipe for French bread, but the section on broccoli shows Julia's new frame of mind. She had always loved broccoli and couldn't resist including it in Volume I, even though it was rarely eaten in France. But she had confined herself to just a few instructions, almost apologetic in tone. In Volume II she stood up and gave it a trumpet fanfare: eight pages of French recipes from *à la polonaise* to timbales—"because this is a book for Americans, and broccoli is one of our best vegetables, and the treatment is à la française," she explained firmly to Simca. (In truth, the charcuterie, the pastries, and the French bread also identify the book as American—nobody in France would dream of making such things at home.) In her next book, *From Julia Child's Kitchen*, she gave herself a truly free hand, right down to an apple betty she christened *pommes Rosemarie*, and she often said this was her favorite book. "Now I don't have to be so damned classic and 'French,'" she exclaimed to Jones. "To hell with that. I am French trained, and I do what I want with my background." Although she continued to trust French technique as the best starting point for any sort of cookery, the distinction between "French" and "not-so-French" was no longer fundamental to her thinking about food. What emerged in its stead were two categories that had been lurking in the shadows until her career caught up with them.

Early in 1961, as she and Simca were winding down their work on Volume I, Julia looked back on some of the issues they had been wrestling with for nearly a decade. "People are always saying WHAT MAKES FRENCH COOKING SO DIFFERENT FROM OTHER NATIONS' COOKING?" she reflected in a letter to Simca, and she set down four principles that struck her as definitive.

> Serious interest in food and its preparation
> Tradition of good cooking . . . which forms French tastes from youth
> Enjoyment of cooking for its own sake—LOVE
> Willingness to take the few extra minutes to be sure things are done as they should be done

Nothing on this list, except for "French tastes," distinguishes French cooking from any other noteworthy cuisine. On the contrary, it's a list that perfectly sums up Julia's outlook on food even when she was most deeply committed to *le gout français*, as she was when she wrote this. Her highest term of culinary praise was never *French*, or *professional*, or *delicious*, though she regularly used such words to describe wonderful food. Her highest praise was the word *serious*—the very first word that came to her fingertips when she started to type these principles. A "serious" cook, to Julia, was a careful, mindful, thoroughly knowledgeable cook, whose pleasure you could taste in the food. Thus her great admiration for Diana Kennedy and Madhur Jaffrey in later years, though she had little interest in Mexican or Indian cooking.

And at the opposite end of the spectrum from the serious cook was the dark angel who hovered over the last principle in the list, the cook who refused to put in those extra minutes it took to reach perfection. This cook—male or female, French or American, famous name or anonymous homebody—was fatally associated with the term *housewife.* Julia never did recover from her early, bruising experiences with that word, and she consistently refused to be associated with such creatures. As she put it many times over the years, whenever the subject of housewives came up, "We are aiming at PEOPLE WHO LIKE TO COOK." Yes, supermarket ingredients could be transformed into authentic French dishes, but not without two ingredients for which there were no substitutes, and Julia named them often: time and love.

Chapter 4

The Performance of Me

WHEN GUESTS CAME to dinner at 103 Irving Street in Cambridge, they spent the whole evening in the kitchen. The table was big and comfortable, and Julia liked having everyone around while she cooked: sometimes she invited people to pick up a knife or a whisk and join in. She would play culinary solos if necessary, but what she really enjoyed was chamber music—everyone on an instrument, chopping garlic or pouring wine or chatting, while a kind of Concerto for Food and Company rose up warm and fragrant in their midst. Cooking alone was very different, though in truth Julia was never really alone at the stove. Long before she cooked on television, she was aware of an audience—first her father and sister, impatient for breakfast as she frantically tossed pancakes and spilled coffee, and later the guests sitting politely in the living room, while she probed the beef with anguish and wondered if it was done, or overdone, or raw. As a bride, she practiced and practiced the role she called chef-hostess until she could give a dinner party without a glitch, or at least without any glitch she couldn't smoothly mend, smiling and conversing all the while. "I always feel it is like putting on a performance, or like live TV or theater—it's got to be right, as there can be no retakes," she told Avis in 1953, nearly a decade before she saw a television camera for the first time. Testing recipes for the book, making the same dish over and over and over, she liked to pretend she was cooking in front of an audience. In part it was a form of culinary discipline, to keep herself from lapsing into casual, unprofessional methods; and in part she just enjoyed the company. When Julia did start cooking in front of a camera, her earliest fans constantly exclaimed over how "natural" she seemed on television, how "real," how "honest," how "homelike." They were right. Performance had long ago become second nature to her.

Her first appearance on television came about shortly after the publication of *Mastering the Art of French Cooking*. She and Paul had decided some years earlier to live in Cambridge after his retirement, and they were still settling into their big clapboard house when Claiborne's rave review appeared. "Presumably, with this puff, we are made!" she wrote jubilantly to Simca. "HOORAY." Later that October, Simca arrived in the United States for the book tour, and the two women—suddenly newsworthy—were invited to be on the *Today* show. Julia wasn't particularly nervous, maybe because she had never heard of it. She and Paul didn't own a television set. But when she learned that four million people would be watching, she knew she needed a plan. "The quickest and most dramatic thing to do in the 5 or 6 minutes allotted to us was to make omelettes," she reported to her sister afterward. "They said they would provide a stove." What they actually provided was a reluctant hot plate, too feeble to heat up properly. But she and Simca brought three dozen eggs to the studio and spent the hour before their time slot practicing. Five minutes before airtime, they started heating up the omelet pan, and by a miracle it was red-hot by the time they needed it. Julia went away very much impressed with the show—everyone was friendly and informal, but the mechanics of the operation were absolutely professional and perfectly timed. It was exactly what she would aim for in her own television shows.

The next TV invitation came along several months later, and this was the one that changed her life. A penciled note is the only thing that remains:

> Beatrice Braude UN4-6400
> WGBH-Chan. 2 CO2-0428
> 84 Mass Ave
> opp MIT
> home = 354 Marlborough St.
> TV

Beatrice Braude was an old friend of the Childs' who had been fired from the USIS in Paris during a McCarthy purge. Now she was working in Boston at WGBH-TV, the fledgling public television station, where she arranged for Julia to be a guest on *I've Been Reading,* a book review program. "They wanted something demonstrated and had a hot plate!" Julia reported to Simca afterward. This time she had a full half hour, so she not only made an omelet, but gave a short lesson in beating egg whites and showed how to cut up vegetables and flute mushrooms. As far as she knew, the only people who saw the program were five of her friends and Jack Savenor, her Cambridge butcher. But twenty-seven ecstatic strangers wrote in to say they loved that woman who did the cooking, and begged the station to bring her back. At WGBH, twenty-seven letters was an avalanche. Startled and impressed, station executives asked Julia to work up a proposal for an entire series on French cooking.

It's possible that *Mastering*, and with it Julia, would have drifted into relative obscurity if she hadn't been discovered by WGBH. She certainly wasn't about to be discovered by anyone else. Even the other stations in what was called educational TV would have been unlikely to take a chance on a plain-faced, middle-aged woman who did difficult cooking with a lot of foreign words in it. But WGBH was in Boston, and that made all the difference. Dozens of colleges and universities, long-standing Brahmin institutions such as the Boston Symphony Orchestra and the Museum of Fine Arts, and an unusually well-educated, well-traveled population made the area unique in the nation. The founders of WGBH intended the new station to be yet another jewel in the city's cultural crown. French cooking fit right in; and, as viewers quickly made clear, so did Julia.

During the summer of 1962, she taped three pilot

programs—omelets, coq au vin, and soufflés—and watched them at home on their new TV. She was horrified to see herself on-screen for the first time, swooping and gasping—"Mrs. Steam Engine," she called herself—but she was determined to master the medium. "The cooking part went OK, but it was the performance of me, as talker and mover, that was not professional," she told Simca. Everything had to be done more slowly, she decided, as if she were under water.

Those pilot programs have been lost, but judging from the letters that poured in to the station, the Julia who ventured in front of the camera that summer had already tapped an instinct for television. "I loved the way she projected over the camera directly to me, the watcher," wrote one of these original fans. "Loved watching her catch the frying pan as it almost went off the counter; loved her looking for the cover of the casserole. It was fascinating to watch her hand motions, which were so firm and sure with the food." Years later, when a friend mentioned that she was about to cook on television for the first time and felt nervous, Julia's advice was simple: "Think about the food." Whether she was flipping an omelet on a hot plate or holding up an unwieldy length of tripe in a beautifully equipped TV kitchen, food was the spark that ignited her performing personality and set it free.

Taping for the series began in January 1963. For her official debut as the "French Chef," Julia chose boeuf bourguignon—a hallmark dish, resonant in her own memory and familiar to anyone who had ever been to a French restaurant. Besides, it was just beef stew. Surely even a housewife couldn't be intimidated by that. And it would illustrate wonderfully well her favorite teaching topic: how French cooking was simply a matter of theme and variations. As soon as home cooks learned to brown beef, deglaze the pan, and set the meat to simmering in wine, they could do the same with lamb, veal, or chicken. Back in the nineteenth century, Julia's long-ago colleagues in domestic science had been equally entranced by the marvelous logic of culinary structure, and were inspired just as she was to make it the basis of their gospel. Of course, they were teaching variations on white sauce, not variations on French stew; but Julia's radiant faith in the message was kin to theirs.

Julia practiced hard: she wrote and rewrote the script, cooked and recooked the stew, figured out the timing for each step of the recipe, plotted her way around the TV kitchen, and tried to memorize the first few sentences she would say. Once the cameras started rolling, they wouldn't stop—the budget didn't allow for breaks and splices—so the show had to be choreographed as tightly as a high-wire act. On Monday evening, February 11, at 8:00 p.m., a large covered casserole appeared on black-and-white television screens across New England, and a breathy voice exclaimed triumphantly, "Boeuf bourguignon! French beef stew in red wine!" A hand lifted the lid from the casserole. "We're going to serve it with braised onions, mushrooms, and wine-dark sauce," the voice went on, lingering fondly over each word in *wine-dark sauce,* while the hand moved a spoon gently through the stew. "A perfectly delicious dish." Then the voice dropped to a mumble—"I'm gonna . . ."—and abruptly stopped. The camera followed the spoon as it emerged from the stew and traveled higher and higher until it reached a mouth. Now a woman's face appeared onscreen, eyes lowered as she leaned intently over the casserole and tasted. Then she straightened up with a satisfied expression, covered the cassserole and put it in the oven, and set a platter of raw meat on the counter. She looked pleasantly into the wrong camera, looked pleasantly into the right camera, closed her eyes for a second, and said, "Hello. I'm Julia Child."

Despite the easygoing warmth that came naturally to her, this debut never quite shook off an air of nervous tension. Julia had no gift for artifice: she could perform, but she couldn't pretend, and not until she turned to the platter of raw beef did she palpably relax. The sight of raw ingredients always restored her equilibrium. "This is called the chuck tender, and it comes from the shoulder blade, up here," she explained, indicating the location on her own body. Apparently the director hadn't expected such a graphic show-and-tell, because the camera remained fixed on the beef. "And this is called the undercut of the chuck, and it's like the continuation of the ribs along here, where it gets up to your neck." Finally, the camera reached her, just in time to see Julia running her hand up her own side. She cut the meat into chunks, chatting comfortably about quantities per person and handling the meat as affectionately as if she were powdering a baby. Then came the browning of the beef, three or four minutes that strikingly illustrated how television—at least as Julia conceived it—could be a great teacher of cooking. Browning is a simple procedure, but there are many more ways to do it wrong than right; and mistakes can ruin the meat. In her methodical way, Julia discussed the pitfalls and how to avoid them, browning the meat properly while an overhead mirror made the contents of the pan clearly visible. To a novice cook, or an experienced cook with bad habits, this lesson would have been life-changing.

After deglazing the pan with wine, she poured the wine over the meat—"just enough liquid so that the meat is barely covered," she instructed, and added tenderly, "It's called *a fleur* in France. When the meat looks like little flowers." Julia had long ago acquired a correct if unmusical French accent, but here she deliberately lapsed into the vulgate. "*A fleur*" became "ah flerr" and "*beurre manie*" came out "burr man-yay," both pronounced in careful Americanese. Perhaps she was trying to sound unpretentious, but she needn't have worried; she was incapable of sounding anything else. In later programs her accent returned to normal.

Here, right at the start of her long career on television, Julia was already recognizably Julia—straightforward, intelligent, relishing the work, and giving star treatment to the food. Her all-important butter dish, the size and shape of a small rowboat, was at the ready; and though she praised her nonstick pan, she made it clear that a nonstick pan was no excuse for cutting back on the butter and oil. Standing at the dining table in the last moments of the show, a ticking clock all but visible in her eyes, she summed up what the program had covered—reminding viewers for at least the third time that they could do lamb, veal, and chicken exactly the same way—and invited them to return for French onion soup next week. She had composed a sign-off—"This is Julia Child, your French Chef. *Bon appétit!*"—but it disintegrated in the flurry of the final seconds. "This is Julia Child, welcome to *The French Chef,* and see you next time," she said, rather confusingly. "*Bon appétit!*"

Throughout the WGBH broadcast area, audiences fell in love. "We have gotten quite a few calls, etc., and people seem to like it," Julia told Koshland after "Boeuf Bourguignon" was aired. "It went quite well, I thought, though a bit rough and hurried in spots." Nobody seemed to mind the rough spots. By March, some six hundred letters had poured in, many asking for the recipes, and others simply expressing rapture. "The station is getting a bit worried as it costs them about 10 cents an answer, but luckily quite a few of the letters enclose contributions to the station. I think we are luckily in at just the right time, as there have been no cooking shows for years, and people are evidently just ripe for them," she wrote to Koshland. Julia often attributed her success to luck and good timing, but the onslaught of mail made it perfectly clear why people responded to *The French Chef:* it was Julia.

. . .

"We love her naturalness & lack of that T.V. manner, her quick but unhurried action, her own appreciation of what she is producing. By the time she gets to the table with her dish and takes off her apron, we are so much 'with' her that we feel as if someone had snatched our plates from in front of us when the program ends."

"I love it where you say, 'Oh, I forgot to tell you thus and so' (so *human* and *consoling* to amateur cooks)."

"You are such a refreshing change from all the dainty cookery and gracious living that women are bombarded with—I hope you live to be a hundred and grow to enormous size."

"Your honesty & forthrightness in all you do and say is greatly appreciated & welcomed in this age of phonyness & half-truths. We love you, Julia!"

"I love your T.V. program! You are the only person I have ever seen who takes a realistic approach to cooking."

"Bernard Berenson wrote that there are two kinds of people, life-diminishing people and life-enhancing people. Certainly you must be the most life-enhancing person in America!"

Julia once said that nineteen hours of preparation went into every half-hour show. First she broke down each recipe into segments, and then she did each step in her kitchen at home while Paul timed her with a stopwatch. How long did it take to chop a sample of onions for onion soup while describing how to hold and use a knife most efficiently, the way chefs did? How long did it take to start the onions cooking in butter and oil? To demonstrate browning the onions with sugar, salt, and flour? To blend stock into the onions and add wine? They worked on each step again and again, trying out different words and phrases, and different ways of showing a particular technique. Then they prepared a script, in the form of a detailed chart displaying time sequences, food, equipment, procedures, and what Julia would say. (Though she worked hard getting the wording as precise as possible, only the very beginning of the show was memorized; the rest she entrusted to adrenaline.) Every single item to be shown or mentioned—oven temperatures, pots of boiling water, samples of asparagus unpeeled and peeled and too scrawny to use, spice jars, spatulas—was listed on the chart in order of discussion. Julia did all the necessary precooking, including a fully prepared version of the dish as well as various ingredients in different stages of readiness. Paul meanwhile created diagrams showing the TV kitchen from Julia's perspective as she faced the camera, with the location of every utensil and every morsel of food.

WORK TOP:

med. chopping knife	bowl of mostly peeled onions	vinegar
paring knife	4 qt. measure	
sharpening steel	empty pie plates	

IN DRAWER:	ON COOK-TOP:
flour bowl	(Left): 2½ qt. empty pan
little metal spatula	(Right): Saucepan of simmering stock
butter dish	" browned onions
	" etuves w/cover
	glass pan of simmering water

IN OVEN: Casserole of gratinéed soup

AVAILABLE: (Left, under): chunk cheese, peeled onion on wax paper

grater, measuring cup w/grated cheese

(Right, under): Pizza-tray w/half loaf Fr. bread, bowl of toasted breads

Conditions in the TV kitchen were primitive: WGBH had burned to the ground two years before, and the new building wasn't finished yet. The first sixty-eight shows were staged in a donated display kitchen at the Cambridge Electric Company, where all the equipment had to be hauled in for rehearsals and taping, then hauled out again. On rehearsal day, Julia and Paul got up at 6:00 a.m. and packed their station wagon with precooked and partially cooked food, raw food, equipment and charts. They also tucked in any special items needed for a particular show, such as the thirty-square-inch chart of a beef carcass that Paul worked on one night until 2:00 a.m., drawing the bone structure and including all the classic cuts of beef. They discovered early on that it was easier to use the fire escape at the electric company than to load and unload the freight elevator, so the two of them carried everything up and set it out on long folding tables. Then Julia and the producer, Ruth Lockwood, rehearsed all day and into the evening, using what Julia called "live food" because that was the only way to get the timing and all the details correct. While they worked, Paul washed mountains of dishes. Then the Childs packed the car, went home, unpacked the car, Julia had a shot of bourbon and made dinner, and they went to bed.

On taping days, they did the same packing and hauling, and while Julia and Ruth were rehearsing, crew members began to arrive, lugging cameras and equipment up the fire escape. The studio became a mass of lights, cameras, and cables. The control center was in a trailer parked around the corner, where director Russ Morash sat watching two screens and issuing instructions to the cameramen. The crew worked out the lighting and camera angles, Julia was made up, and a microphone was hooked to the inside of her blouse, with a wire running down her left leg and into an electrical outlet. (By a miracle, she never tripped over this tether.) Finally, the floor manager shouted, "Sixty seconds! Quiet in the studio!" Julia looked into the camera, and taping began. Afterward, the crew devoured all the cooked food and took a break, while Paul washed dishes. Then the kitchen was set up with all different food and equipment, and a second show was taped. Bourbon and dinner followed.

The schedule was relentless, and despite the hours of rehearsal, those twenty-eight minutes were harrowing. One day the studio was so hot that after they completed the run-through, the butter was put into the refrigerator instead of being placed in the drawer where Julia was supposed to find it at the proper time. When the time came, she told Simca, "All I found was a little bowl with a paper in it saying 'butter.' So I had to say, 'Merde alors, forgot the butter, always forget something,' and go practically off camera to the frig. And I pull out the butter carton and find to my horror it has only about 30 grams of butter in it. Luckily I was able to spot when one camera was off me and focusing on the chicken, and was able to mouth an anguished 'BUTTER' to the floor manager, who snuck into the frig, with trembling fingers peeled paper off a piece of butter, and snuck it on the work table, with no camera spotting him." The production team used to say they aged ten years with each show. But over the years, only a handful of shows had to be redone because of accidents or mistakes Julia couldn't fix on the spot. The second show, on onion soup, was one she couldn't save: she swept through the recipe so quickly that she arrived at the dining table with seven minutes to fill with chat instead of two. After that experience, they worked out a system of what they called "idiot cards"—nearly one a minute, tracking the time and reminding Julia what she was supposed to say and do. ASPARAGUS. SET TIMER. HOW BUY, STORE. FRONT BURNER HOT. (The camera she was supposed to be looking into sometimes wore a small hat and a sign: ME FRIEND.) Later a second set of cards, orange instead of white, was introduced for emergencies. If Julia forgot an ingredient, or described a pot as "aluminum-covered steel" instead of "enamel-covered steel," Ruth Lockwood would flash a special orange card alerting her to the error, and Julia would make the correction.

Six months into it, Julia was getting quite good, Paul reported to his brother. "Now she wipes the sweat off her face only when the close-up camera is concentrating briefly on the subsiding foam in the sauté-pan, for example. Her pacing is steady rather than rush-here and hold-there. She knows how to signal the Director that she's going to make a move out of range of the cameras, so they can follow, by saying, 'Now I'm going to go to the oven to check-up on the soufflé'—instead of suddenly darting out of the picture toward the oven." WGBH continued to be overrun with letters from enchanted viewers. The *Boston Globe* published an editorial calling the show "the talk of New England" and signed up Julia as a regular columnist in the food pages. Kitchenware stores found they were running out of items Julia used on the show—flan rings one week, oval casseroles the next. "I can hardly go out of the house now without being accosted in the street," Julia told Koshland in some amazement. New York, San Francisco, Sacramento, Philadelphia, Washington, and Pittsburgh all picked up the show, and floods of mail poured into every new station as soon as Julia appeared on-screen. Stories ran in *Time*, *Newsweek*, the *Saturday Evening Post*, and *TV Guide.* By January 1965, all ninety stations on the public television network were carrying *The French Chef*, and WGBH found it could raise money for the station every week by selling tickets to the taping sessions at $5 apiece. Paul greeted the audience before each session and asked them please not to laugh aloud during the show.

Julia spent most of the next forty years on television—new programs and repeats, public television and commercial TV, season-long series and one-time specials. She was a star, a host, a guest, a commentator, and a voice-over; once, to the delight of millions including herself, she was evoked by Dan Ackroyd on *Saturday Night Live* in a skit that became a classic. (Hacking away at a chicken, he fatally cut himself and collapsed, shrieking, "Save the liver!") She grew old on camera: the energetic teacher who whipped up an entire beef Wellington in a half hour gave way over the years to an elderly woman who charmed the audience while letting guest chefs do most of the cooking. But her lasting image was established in the 1960s and 1970s by *The French Chef.* This was the Julia who won a permanent place in the nation's memory bank.

The self-consciousness that fluttered through the "Boeuf Bourguignon" show quickly disappeared with experience, but Julia retained a real-world quality that television couldn't tame. Even the food seemed to be a live, spontaneous participant. Julia welcomed it warmly and gave everything she had to the relationship—parrying with the food, letting it surprise and delight her, very nearly bantering with it. Sometimes she lifted a cleaver and made a fine show of whacking the food to pieces, as if they had both agreed beforehand that the end happily justified the means. The day she made bouillabaisse, she placed a massive fish head on the counter and kept it there by her side, one great bulging eye staring out at the camera, while she prepared the stock. Every now and then she found a reason to pick up the gigantic head and fondle it. Tasting, of course, was a recurring event in each program, each taste a cameo moment treasured by the camera. Julia's whole countenance shut down as she lifted the spoon and focused inward, then she opened up again and, most often, looked pleased. "Mmm, that's good." And if there was a chance to nibble, she unabashedly nibbled. After a painstaking demonstration of how to fold the egg whites into the chocolate batter for a *reine de Saba* cake, she held up the spatula and announced, "We have this little bit on the edge of the spatula which is for the cook." Avidly, she licked up the raw batter—a treat as old as cake baking—and added, "That's part of the recipe."

Julia never said cooking was easy, but she said many times that anybody could learn it who wanted to. Viewers following her through the steps of a recipe could see for themselves how the consistency of a batter changed as the eggs were added, could watch the chocolate melting safely over a pan of hot water, could read the confidence in her motions as she snipped the gills off a sunfish with shears, or plunged a lobster headfirst into boiling water. Nothing was left unsaid, very little was relegated to instinct. Often she tossed in salt or spices without using a measuring spoon, but she always knew the exact amounts and mentioned them. "Here's what half a teaspoon of salt looks like," she said once, and poured it into her hand to show people. She was teaching people to use their senses when they cooked, because she thought the senses belonged in every well-run kitchen, like good knives. There was no better instrument in the service of accuracy than an attentive cook who was watching and smelling and tasting. Monitoring the progress of a syrup for candied orange peel, she made a point of listening for the "boiling sound" coming from the mixture. You can use a thermometer here, she told viewers, "but I think it's a good thing to see and feel how it is."

Cooking shows had been a staple of early television, but none of them bore any resemblance to *The French Chef*. Most were plain-spun, local broadcasts featuring a home economist or food editor. James Beard and Dione Lucas, two of the best-known culinary authorities before Julia's arrival on the scene, had starred in their own cooking programs, but neither of these experts was able to develop the skill or personality demanded by the screen. Their shows left no mark on the medium. By the 1960s, cooking had been relegated to the dim wastes of daytime TV, where it reveled in the simpleminded sentiments considered appropriate for housewives. Julia's real peers were those beloved figures who made instant, indelible impressions in the first decades of television—Lucille Ball, Steve Allen, Milton Berle. Yet she stood out here, too, because what she was doing on-screen didn't fit any existing categories. She invented no character, staged no formal entertainments; her original show didn't even carry her name, and the point of the half hour over which she presided was to teach, not to focus attention on herself. In fact, Julia spent her first decade on TV begging WGBH to put guest chefs on *The French Chef* with her because she thought people would learn much more if they could be exposed to a wide range of teachers. (The station never complied, first because the program was so experimental, and later because it was so clearly and magnificently Julia's show.) Despite the modesty that was intrinsic to her personality, the camera adored her, perhaps because she generally forgot about it as soon as the food absorbed her attention. Often she looked straight into the camera and gave a sudden little smile, because Ruth Lockwood had been holding up an idiot card that read SMILE. In a medium stoked by artificiality and blandness almost from the beginning, Julia was herself and famous for it.

At the same time, however, she tended her public image with great care. Paul did all the still photography for *The French Chef* and tried to make sure that his were the only photographs of Julia that appeared in the press. She was not conventionally good-looking or particularly photogenic, and newspaper photographers weren't going to edit their contact sheets as painstakingly as he did. As he told his brother, "The image can be spoiled by letting out half a dozen stinkers." Over the years, similarly, she went on many diets but rarely discussed them in public until late in her career. What she preferred to tell the press, when reporters invariably asked how she controlled her weight in the face of so much tempting food, was that she and Paul simply watched their calories and tried never to have second helpings. (But, "TOO FAT!" she groaned to an old friend. "I'm just too damned fat, my waist is middle aged, my bust is bulging bubbidom, and [worst of all], I really can't buy any clothes anymore.") A few years after she started on television, she bought her first wig—"which will save a pile of distress in rainy weather," Paul explained—and in the late 1960s, she had plastic surgery for the first time, an "eye job." In the spring of 1971, she had a complete face-lift. The operation took place in Paris so that she could go straight to their house in Provence to recuperate in absolute privacy. When she learned that Simca was planning to be next door in her house at the same time—Simca would be working with an American writer who was translating her cookbook into English—Julia insisted that the translating be done elsewhere or at another time. "You forget, ma chérie, that I am, malgré tout, a public figure and it will not do to have a reporter and writer be aware in any way of my condition," she wrote to her colleague. "I am sorry to be difficult about this, but you must understand the problem!" Nobody knew about the face-lift—"my sacquepage," Julia called it—except Paul, Simca, and Ruth

Lockwood. "People think I look just fine, and so rested," she wrote to Simca after returning home. "Avis said your skin looks so good, and your face—I said, well, since the TV I've learned how to put on makeup. Actually, it is very subtle—the neck fixed, the pouches at either side of the chin, and the hollows out of the cheeks. I didn't realize myself until suddenly I looked—no turkey neck! No dewlaps!" She had plastic surgery again in 1977 and once more in 1989.

But her image was a bigger project than simply the condition of her face and figure. Soon after *The French Chef* became a local sensation, Julia began to get invitations—Would she appear at a department store and demonstrate cooking? Would she appear at a charity fund-raiser? Would she endorse this product, use this equipment on air, plug this restaurant? Early on, she made it a rule to say no to everything except charitable ventures. "I just don't want to be in any way associated with commercialism (except for selling the book in a dignified way), and don't want to get into the realm of being a piece of property trotting about hither and yon," she told Koshland. "The line is sometimes difficult to see, but I know where I mean it to be." Anytime she accepted a fee for a cooking demonstration or a special appearance, she donated the money to WGBH. If viewers wrote to ask where she bought her mixer, or what brand of rum she was using, she wrote back with the information, but she never mentioned a brand name in public. Thanks to the success of her books, as well as an inheritance, she and

Paul didn't need the money; and she often said how grateful she was to be able to turn down such offers. But she made her stance for another reason as well. Commercial endorsements were demeaning: they tarnished the reputation of the cook. James Beard lent his name to many food companies, always justifying it by saying he needed the money, and Julia felt that his standing in the profession was suffering as a result. Audiences understood the difference between paid-for and unfettered speech; they loved her for staying on the right side of the line, and she had no intention of letting them down by muddying what she called "the purest of noncommercial images."

With the help of her lawyer when necessary, Julia kept her name free of commercial taint throughout her career. But other aspects of her public image had a way of tripping her up, often right on air. Scrupulous though she was about how she looked and how she taught, Julia was so comfortably at home whenever she was handling food that she moved around the TV kitchen as if she were in her own house. She stashed away the colander and then forgot where it was, hunted about for the mixing fork, lost track of a casserole; once she snatched up a huge handful of paper towels and swabbed her face, explaining, "I've got so many burners on here, I'm hot." No matter how well she planned a program, moreover, reality had a way of breaking over the proceedings like a raw egg. Julia's equanimity in the face of a crisis was dazzling—repairing the molded potatoes that stuck to the bottom of the pan, withstanding a series of electrical shocks from the microphone tucked in her blouse (she did keep fiddling anxiously with the mic, but she never stopped teaching), shoving aside a spoon holder that had fallen over with a crash, ignoring a scraper that flew from her grasp, and dismissing the collapse of a frosting-laden "twig" in the Yule log by remarking, "Well, I guess that would happen in a forest, anyway. Things sitting there a long time, and they begin losing their strength." When she unmolded a *tarte tatin*, only to see it collapse into a messy heap of apples with the crust slipping off to the side, she simply said, "That was a little loose. But I'll just have to show you that it's not going to make too much of a difference, because it's all going to fix up." Rapidly she tucked the apples together on top of the crust, then carried the disheveled tart into the dining room along with another "ready" tart that had been unmolded perfectly earlier in the day. "Now everybody can get one of each tart," she said as she cut slices, managing despite everything to sound like a chemistry teacher showing the results of an experiment that went off just as it was supposed to. "There. I think that actually makes a more interesting dessert."

One day Julia taped a program with four different potato recipes, trying to move through them at a good pace. Standing at the stove over a large mashed potato cake in a skillet, she waited a little impatiently for the cake to brown on the bottom. She eyed the pan and shook it dubiously, then decided to try to flip the cake over anyway. Clearly she knew she was taking a chance. "When you flip anything, you just have to have the courage of your convictions, particularly if it's sort of a loose mass, like this." She gave the pan a swift, practiced jerk. The potato cake rose heavily into the air and disintegrated, half of it spilling in shreds onto the stove. "Well, that didn't go very well," she observed steadily. "You see, when I flipped it, I didn't have the courage to do it the way I should have." Quickly she gathered up the pieces and reassembled them in the pan. "You can always pick it up," she remarked as she worked. "You're alone in the kitchen—who is going to see? But the only way you learn how to flip things is just to flip them."

"You're alone in the kitchen—who is going to see?" This incident became legendary and then apocryphal, revised so many times in the telling that the original event disappeared. Julia dropped a chicken, Julia dropped two chickens, she dropped a turkey, a twenty-five-pound turkey, a pig, a duck, and in each case blithely returned them to their platters—all fantasies, but people recalled them joyfully. They also remembered seeing Julia pour wine into a dish, then finish off the bottle herself, saying, "One of the rewards of being a cook." Actually, she had been showing how to juice tomatoes and finished the lesson by drinking up the last bit of juice; but memory preferred wine. "Sometimes she forgets to put the seasoning in the ragout; sometimes she drops a turkey in the sink," wrote Lewis Lapham in the *Saturday Evening Post.* "In New York's Greenwich Village . . . a coterie of avant-garde painters and musicians gathers each week in a loft to watch *The*

French Chef, convinced that Mrs. Child is far more diverting than any professional comedian." A story in *Time* played up her "muddleheaded nonchalance"; a piece in *TV Guide* reported "blunders," "grunts," and "mutters." "Practically every article on Julie so far has concentrated on the clown instead of the woman, the cook, the expert or the revolutionary," Paul complained to his brother. Julia hadn't intended to do kitchen vaudeville, but that was the image taking shape—despite the fact that efficiency and competence characterized her television cooking far more accurately than pratfalls did.

Reading the fan mail as well as the press, Julia could see that the informality and humor that came so naturally were doing just what she wanted the show to do: dispel the fog of intimidation around French cooking. Hence she was willing to play up the entertainment aspect of the program, especially in the opening moments—sorting through mounds of tangled seaweed to reveal a twenty-pound lobster, for instance, or standing over a chorus line of six raw chickens exclaiming, "Julia Child presents the chicken sisters! Miss Broiler! Miss Fryer! Miss Roaster! Miss Caponette! Miss Stewer! And old Madame Hen!" But she was of two minds about the bloopers. They were peerless teaching tools: every cook ran into mishaps, and Julia knew that to see the *pommes Anna* stuck helplessly to the bottom of the pan, then rescued and restored, constituted a more memorable lesson than the original would have been. "It may well happen to you," she always told viewers as she patched and revised. But she hated making mistakes in public. Informality was one thing; ruining the food was definitely another. And she didn't want to be known as a bumbling clown; she wanted to be known as a good, professional cook. When hapless beginners wrote to her begging for advice—which they did in such numbers that she composed a form letter to send in response—she was full of sympathy and encouragement, but never admitted having been in the same position herself. "The story of the beginner cook is often a real tale of woe, and I feel for her," she told them. "Whenever *I* sew or knit it turns out a disaster. I really think the best thing is to take some cooking lessons. . . . Cooks are made, geniuses are born, and you can learn to cook with the right instruction—especially if you are lucky enough to be married to someone who loves good food, as that will always inspire you." It was, of course, her own story, minus the early agony.

"*Bon courage!*" she bid the audience at the end of the flopped-potato-cake show. Be of good courage! "*Courage!*" she said again, after a visibly exhausting bout with French bread. When she demonstrated the nerve-racking process of creating a lacy caramel "cage" to go over a cake, she didn't try to disguise the challenge: she told viewers to fail if they must, and try again. "Cooking is one failure after another, and that's how you finally learn," she told the audience while she stirred the caramel. "You've got to have what the French call '*je m'enfoutisme,*' or 'I don't care what happens—the sky can fall and omelets can go all over the stove, I'm going to learn.'" It was the chief lesson she had gleaned from her own cooking failures, which dogged her long after she had learned to cook. "I must say I find myself often in the embarrassing position of being the much publicized visiting supreme authority on culinary matters, and then laying an egg on top of it," she wrote to Avis in 1953, after a Christmas visit to friends during which she botched the timing of a turkey. The next year she truffled and stuffed a turkey, then overcooked it, burned the broiled endive, nearly forgot the salad dressing, and was late with the coffee. "How miserable, depressing, and slapping-down such a fiasco is, is it not?" Nearly a decade later, living in Cambridge as the lionized author of *Mastering the Art of French Cooking*, she entertained her new friend James Beard and, she told Simca, "cooked the worst dinner of my life." An elaborate preparation of veal scallops—cognac, Madeira, truffles—lacked flavor, and she didn't know why; the broccoli was underdone, and so were the sautéed potatoes; and the chocolate cake tasted terrible. ("Don't ever use Baker's unsweetened chocolate for anything!") Beard didn't seem to mind the meal: he promptly invited her to teach at his school in New York.

Mistakes were bad enough at a dinner party for friends, but when she fumbled on television, the moment was captured forever on tape—and shown over and over in reruns. She knew audiences cherished the near disasters, but she longed for more control; she longed to present a more polished performance. "If we had more money, it would be so useful to overshoot and be able to edit out with dissolves to indicate time lapses—and no pretense that it is a live show," she told Ruth Lockwood. *The French Chef* never progressed to that level, in part because the production team was determined to keep the show from becoming too slick, although with the advent of color and a new studio kitchen, the show looked far more dressed up by the time the last programs were taped in 1972. With the two series that followed—*Julia Child & Company* and *Julia Child & More Company*—Julia was able to move a good deal closer to the image she preferred. These programs, produced on a bigger budget with all the benefits of technology, were staged in a bright, chic kitchen without a trace of home to it: the sheen was pure television, and Julia herself seemed to revel in the artificiality. Perhaps because it was possible at last to do retakes, she was more relaxed and never looked as though she were lunging for her next words. Her relationship with the food remained as high spirited as ever—shaking a pan of cucumbers, slapping the dough on the counter, admiring the teeth on a gigantic monkfish, adding "homemade chicken stock, as you can see" as she poured it from a can. But if the tension that often marked *The French Chef* was gone, so, alas, was the gratifying sight of the unpredictable, leaping out of a bowl or skillet to test the mettle of the heroine.

For reasons nobody seemed able to explain, the *Company* series didn't make much of an impact when they were first aired. WGBH admitted later that it had done a poor job of promoting and distributing *More Company*, which wasn't seen at all in New York until it went into reruns. Julia had been a familiar presence on television for more than fifteen years and was considered a national treasure, but while critics and many of her fans were happy with the new shows—and the reruns went on forever—the initial ratings and publicity came nowhere near those of *The French Chef.* "I am quite aware that there comes a time when one is frankly out of style, out of step, and had better fold up and steal away," Julia had acknowledged years earlier, as she foresaw *The French Chef* drawing to a close. "However, I shall certainly hang on with full vigor for the time being." She was still vigorous, but the experience with *Company* persuaded her that if she wanted to keep going, she had to take her television career in a different direction. Like any artist, she was far more interested in the future than in settling back to read her old reviews. In 1980, she withdrew from the shelter of WGBH and began a long association with *Good Morning America,* her first regular commitment to commercial television. The two-and-a-half-minute cooking segments were enormously popular, and she relished the format for its efficiency, as well as for the huge new audience it delivered. By 1983, when shooting began on her next public television series, she had established her own production company, which meant she could exert much greater control over her own programs than she ever had before. She still thought of herself primarily as a teacher, but she was convinced that she had to package herself with far more glitz if her message was going to get out.

The idea for the new series, which she developed with director Russ Morash, was to offer not a cooking school show but a television magazine, glossy and expensive. Julia would do a bit of cooking, but she would also visit fisheries, farms, cheese makers, and vineyards, chat with guest chefs, and welcome guests to a luxurious party that would conclude each program. Home base for the show would be a twenty-five-acre ranch near Santa Barbara, and Julia would have hair, makeup, and wardrobe professionals outfitting her for each program. As a coproduction of WGBH and Julia's own company, the new series would be, as her business manager put it, "quintessentially Julia's own show."

Dinner at Julia's was a disaster, the only real embarrassment in her long career. Julia looked grotesque, her hair frizzed and her makeup garish, dressed up in caftans and evening pajamas, or rigged out for a barbecue in jeans, a vest, and a purple ten-gallon hat. Though she was never ill at ease, she had little of substance to do in her long stretches of time on camera. As she stood there listening to a winemaker or chocolatier describe how various products were made, she looked as if she were a cardboard replica of herself, deployed to lend the symbolic presence of Julia Child to an alien landscape. With the food, as always, she was restored to life, but the cooking sequences were designed to show only quick highlights from the preparation of a dish, not an entire recipe. Nothing that happened on-screen was alive or spontaneous; nature itself had been banished. Even the chanterelles in the mushroom-gathering sequence had been carefully tucked into the ground by hand, before the cameras arrived. The sumptuous mansion, the Rolls-Royce pulling up to the door, the staged parties with their make-believe guests pretending to have fun—it was a painful spectacle, and Julia's fans were appalled. The reviews were lacerating, and the letters were worse. "To see this darling, feisty, gifted lady dressed up in cowboy clothes, tottering around in boots, swishing among rather wooden-looking 'guests,' and above all to see her modest, perfect little show given the Beverly Hills treatment, the ostentation, the waiters, the gratuitous free plugs for restaurants and grape-growers, cheese factories, and what not, well, it's awful!" "I miss my old friend Julia." "We want you to be human." "How *could* you?"

Julia never apologized, any more than she did when she had to serve a soufflé fallen flat. "We had such a good time making those shows" was all she would say when a reporter asked her how she felt about the debacle. But it was another ten years before she returned to television with a new series, and this time she stayed on the sidelines. *Cooking with Master Chefs* featured sixteen chefs preparing meals in their home kitchens, and Julia—who called herself Alistaire Cookie and wished the series could be named *Masterpiece Cooking*—introduced each show. The only complaints about the program were that people wanted to see more of Julia. After that, she made sure to share the screen with her guests, acting as a personable interlocutor as they cooked; and the last three series she made—*Cooking at Home with*

Master Chefs, *Baking with Julia*, and her duet with Jacques Pépin, *Julia and Jacques: Cooking at Home*—were all taped in the kitchen at 103 Irving Street. It was the right formula: old fans were satisfied, new ones were smitten, and *Dinner at Julia's* faded from public memory.

Back in 1942, when Julia belonged to a team of volunteers who watched the skies over Southern California for enemy aircraft, a story in the local paper noted that members of the group habitually called each other "Mr." or "Mrs.," with one exception—"Julia McWilliams, whom everybody addresses as Julia." Decades later, people were still addressing her as Julia. In person or on-screen, her whole countenance invited familiarity; barriers dropped away as if she had been a friend forever. Paul used to marvel at a phenomenon he witnessed again and again while they were living in Paris: he called it *"la Julification des gens"*—"the Julia-fication of everybody." She had a way of hypnotizing people, he once said, "so they open up like flowers in the sun." Nobody was insensible to her effect: one of the themes that ran through the piles and piles of mail was pure gratitude. "Thank you for being such a pleasure." "Many thanks for bringing so much pleasure." Or, as a thirteen-year-old put it, "I don't know why, but whenever I see you it makes me feel good." Hard as she worked on her image, in the end it was irrelevant. "You are so utterly real, I feel as if I know you," a fan wrote. They did know her, perfectly.

Chapter 5

Real Male Men

JULIA LOVED PAUL, and she also loved their marriage, which seemed to her the highest form of life. "We are a team," she often said. "We do everything together." To be part of a team was her favorite way to work—she always referred fondly to the "team" of cooks and technicians involved in her television series, or the "team" of editors and artists producing a cookbook—and the team at the heart of it all was Julia and Paul. Whenever she talked about her career, she said "we," not "I," and she meant it literally. Paul attended all business meetings and participated in all decisions, helped rework the recipes for television, hauled equipment, washed dishes, took photographs, created designs and graphics, peeled and chopped and stirred, ran errands, read the mail and helped answer it, wrote the dedications in all her books, accompanied her on publicity tours and speaking engagements, sat with her at book signings, took part in most of her press interviews, provided the wine expertise, baked baguette after baguette during the French bread experiments, and in general made a point of being at her side on all occasions, professional or social. Yet he was self-sufficient. When he wasn't needed—because Julia was at work in the kitchen with Simca, for instance, or rehearsing with Ruth Lockwood—he disappeared happily into his own world, painting and photographing and gardening. In the firmament of useful, devoted spouses who serve celebrity without a trace of malevolence, he was one of the few husbands.

Paul had no qualms about living with powerful, independent women. His mother had been a singer and soloist who worked for a living; and the first love of his life, Edith Kennedy, was a single mother some twenty years older than he who regularly attracted acolytes to her Cambridge salon. Julia had no such distinctions when he met her, but she was certainly bigger, and far more skilled at relating to people. Being married to a woman who outranked him physically and personally never bothered Paul, and he was deeply grateful for what Julia gave him. He knew he had a streak of grouchiness, that he tended to be solitary, and that Julia had warmed and gentled him. "I am continuously conscious of my good fortune in living with her," he wrote to his brother from Paris in 1953. "I hate to think what a sour old reprobate I might have been without that face to look at." Occasionally, after a taping of *The French Chef,* while Paul was collecting dirty dishes and the audience was crowding worshipfully around Julia, he thought back to their foreign service days. "It was, 'Monsieur Child, l'Attaché Culturel des Etats Unis!'—and some minutes later: 'ah oui, et voilà aussi Mme. Child.'" ("Mr. Child, the

U.S. Cultural Attaché! Oh yes, and here's Mrs. Child, too.") He enjoyed the reversal, he told his brother: "I feel Nature is restoring an upset balance."

The fact that the world paid little attention to his art, his poems were consistently rejected by magazines, and most of his published photographs were of Julia didn't appear to trouble him. Standing by at a book signing with nothing to do while "Julia's adoring public" swarmed over her, he felt he was providing a service just by being there. "It demonstrated that Julia is part of a combination rather than a lone operator," he explained. "I remember how horrid it was for Edith. Financially & sexually rapacious men were constantly trying to take advantage of her. My plan is *never* to have Julia appear anywhere in public without the very evident husband." For Paul to experience such a rush of masculine satisfaction in this role—self-appointed protector of a giant—says much about the confidence he brought to his marriage. He called her "Joooolie" or sometimes "my little wifelet," created the witty, loving Valentines they sent out every year instead of Christmas cards ("Wish you were here," read one of them, showing Paul and Julia in a bubble bath), and considered her the most remarkable and delightful creature on earth. Every morning they liked to snuggle in bed together for a half hour after the alarm went off, and at the end of the day, Paul would read aloud from *The New Yorker* while Julia made dinner. "We are never not together," Paul said once, contentedly. One evening after the dishes were washed, Julia stayed in the kitchen and made an impromptu batch of blueberry muffins. When they came out of the oven, Paul opened a bottle of vintage Veuve Clicquot for a late-night celebration. What was the occasion? Just life. Or as Paul explained it, "Iced champagne and hot blueberry muffins!"

Paul was one of the few men of his generation who found it natural, even admirable, for women to have careers. It wouldn't have occurred to him to object to his wife's passion for work, even as it swept her from cooking school to teaching to writing to national television. But during their years in Europe, both of them took it for granted that Paul's job came first. As a foreign service couple, they were expected to socialize and entertain a great deal, and Julia's participation counted heavily. More important, at least from Julia's point of view, was the fact that Paul worked extremely hard and needed all the moral and logistical support she could give him. This posed no problems for her during the first years of their marriage, when her only obligation was to be Mrs. Paul Child—a job she treasured, especially in the entrancing new surroundings of their life in Paris. "The husband comes home for lunch," she told Avis. "I love that!" But the more deeply involved she became in the cookbook project, the more she resented being pulled away for consular events, tea with the embassy wives, and Paul's occasional trips. He hated to travel without her, and she hated to make him unhappy, so she often went along despite a kitchen full of eggs or mushrooms pleading for her attention. "My first job is wifedom," she said resignedly, in the midst of an unwanted burst of official travel right after they moved to Marseille. When she couldn't bear to leave the book, she sent him off alone and felt horribly guilty about it. "If I was able to put in as much work as I would like to, we would soon be having a divorce, I fear," she told Simca, exaggerating the potential for divorce, but not the painful sense of conflict. Though she was sorry to leave France for their posting in Germany, she welcomed at least one aspect of the new assignment. "Paul doesn't come home for lunch, and I shall have almost the whole day to work in," she reported to Avis. "Thank heaven!"

Much as she cherished wifedom, it was impossible for Julia to be Paul's helpmate and nothing else. And much as Paul believed in her career, what he really wanted was to have Julia with him at all times. To be pulled in such implacably opposite directions was a source of constant distress for her. Again and again she vowed to be a more dedicated diplomatic wife, only to find herself back in the depths of the manuscript, reflecting mournfully, "I am a cook book." So when Paul began planning his retirement from the foreign service, they decided what would suit them both best would be a quiet, companionable future in Cambridge. Paul would paint, Julia would give cooking lessons—perhaps two a week. If the book became a success, maybe she could break into magazine food writing. Paul could take the photographs for her stories. Life would be simple and harmonious. Then came *The French Chef*, and any dreams of domestic balance shattered as Julia's new career crashed like a meteor into the center of their marriage. New roles sprang up and grabbed them—she the star and he the support staff—but they were determined to maintain what Julia called "that lovely intertwining of life, mind, and soul that a good marriage is." She knew the TV schedule was hard on Paul, who missed concerts and art galleries and dinners with friends, as well as time for his own pursuits. In 1965, her royalties from the book enabled them to build La Pitchoune, the little Provençal house on Simca's property near Grasse; and they retreated there often for a cozier, less pressured daily life. But the real reason their marriage flourished despite the frantic demands they placed on it was that they came up with a very traditional arrangement, albeit with a twist of their own. Paul and Julia agreed to live one life, and that life would be Julia's.

Despite, or perhaps because of, this arrangement, Julia sometimes professed loyalty to old-fashioned gender assignments. "I think the role of a woman is to be married to a nice man and enjoy her home," Julia told the *New York Times* in 1966. "She must have something outside to keep conversation going and herself alert, but I can't think of anything nicer than homemaking." Even the reporter was unconvinced—she called it a "simplistic" viewpoint—and it certainly lacked any roots in Julia's desires, beliefs, or experiences. Apart from cooking, housework bored her, and she was appalled by the Pasadena wives who lounged on their patios and played bridge all day. But she identified so strongly as a wife, she barely noticed that it was Paul who played that part in their marriage. At the time of this interview, moreover, the women's movement was gathering steam; and Julia worried that cooking might be jettisoned, especially her kind of labor-intensive cooking. Betty Friedan had made it clear in *The Feminine Mystique* that women had responsibilities in the world, not just in the kitchen. Julia didn't disagree, but she wanted to make sure the kitchen received the time and respect it was due. She was also aware that she still had something of a housewife problem. Her recipes could seem very intimidating, especially in print, and she relied on book sales for most of her earned income, not the nominal fees of public television. Associating herself with ordinary domestic life was an important aspect of her image. In later interviews over the years, she gave firm support to women with careers and spoke out vigorously in favor of abortion rights; nonetheless she always insisted she wasn't a feminist. "I just think that women should be treated as people," she said. So do feminists, but Julia was constitutionally unable to be a camp follower, no matter what the camp was.

If her proclamation of faith in homemaking rang a bit false, her faith in marriage did not: this was a belief at the core of her being. Julia changed much more than her name when she married: she changed her very identity, from an individual to half of a couple. She was Julia of Paul and Julia, fundamentally incomplete on her own, one piece of a two-part jigsaw puzzle. And once she became a wife, it was from that perspective that she viewed the world. People belonged in pairs, she felt—male and female together, marching through life as if they were streaming aboard the ark.

For this reason, she found homosexuality outlandish—not immoral, and certainly not to be criminalized, but a rude disruption in the natural order of things. Homophobia was a socially acceptable form of bigotry in mid-century America, and Julia and Paul participated without shame for many years. She often used the term *pedal* or *pedalo*—French slang for homosexual—draping it with condescension, pity, and disapproval. "I had my hair permanented at E. Arden's, using the same *pedalo* I had before (I wish all the men in OUR profession in the USA were not *pedals*!)," she wrote to Simca. Fashion designers were "that little bunch of Pansies," a cooking school was "a nest of homo-vipers," a Boston dinner party was "peopled by 3 fags in an expensive house. . . . We felt hopelessly square and left when decently possible," and San Francisco was beautiful but full of *pedals*—"It appears that SF is their favorite city! I'm tired of them, talented though they are." The opposite of homosexual, in her terminology, was "normal" or "well muscled" or "very masculine!" Or, as she often put it, "real male men." Lesbianism was less of an affront to her, though she felt sorry for women so sexually benumbed that they were not attracted to men. ("Can't be much fun.")

It appears never to have struck Julia that she was talking about homosexuals the way her father talked about Jews, blacks, foreigners, intellectuals, and artists. All her adult life, his prejudices had sickened her, especially because he was so contemptuous of Paul, who represented several categories of humanity that John McWilliams despised. Her father's ugly convictions threw Paul into such a rage that he finally stopped visiting Pasadena with her. Yet she was able to detest her father's bigotry while her own remained a blind spot. During the McCarthy era—the period when her liberalism was forged, mostly out of sheer outrage—Paul himself was summoned to Washington from Germany, on suspicion of being a Communist and a homosexual. He was interrogated for a day, then cleared. (The only evidence for the first charge was his acquaintance with a couple of other people whose politics were under investigation. As for his supposed homosexuality, the most damaging evidence seemed to be the fact that he was married. As his interrogators pointed out, many homosexuals were married and had children.) Paul laughed outright at the accusation, and Julia did the same when she reported the incident to Avis. "Homosexuality. Haw Haw. Why don't they ask the wife about that one?" Even the knowledge that McCarthy, whom Julia regarded as evil personified, was using the specter of homosexuality as a deadly weapon, didn't raise any alarms in her own conscience.

For all her prejudice, however, when she met homosexuals whose appearance and body language were what she called "normal," or straight, much of her disapproval evaporated. What she really disliked was effeminacy in men—a caricature that made it clear how they spurned the male-female differences and rituals she so relished. "My, I hate being a widow!" she exclaimed to Avis when Paul was summoned away from Germany for the investigation. "And I have finally had to admit to myself that if I were a real widow, I'd probably have to take to the streets. It's just no fun; it is not only the physical male, but the mental male. Thank god there are two sexes, is all I can say." Julia's whole being was ignited by proximity to men: they were at the center of her world view, and their presence lent energy, authority, and dignity to all undertakings. The very idea of a social or professional event designed around women was offensive to her. "I hate groups of women," she said many times, flatly and without apology. No matter the occasion, if it was only for women, she was convinced it would resemble a Helen Hokinson cartoon in *The New Yorker:* silly clubwomen dithering over their agendas. As a foreign service wife, of course, she was invited to countless ladies' luncheons and tea parties; they drove her wild with boredom, especially when the cookbook manuscript was waiting back home. "I just cannot stand to waste a day like that anymore," she told Simca after an endless afternoon of female socializing. "And if there is anything I HATE, it is a ladies tea parlor." The only women's events she approved of were meetings of Les Gourmettes, because everyone was busy with the important work of cooking and eating. Otherwise, "Cackle-cackle . . . sounds like a hen house" was her invariable reaction to being in a room full of females. In 1973, she was one of a dozen Women of the Century honored at a lavish dinner and spent the evening talking with Lillian Hellman, Marya Mannes, Louise Nevelson, and Pauline Trigère, among others. It was very nice, she remarked later, but they should have invited some men. She said the spark was missing.

Not surprisingly, when clubs and restaurants that excluded women came under pressure from feminists to change their policies, Julia sided with the men. "I am very much against the new policy at the Ritz of allowing unaccompanied women into the Grill," she told an audience at the all-male St. Botolph Club in Boston, where she had been invited to give a talk. "They'll turn it into a clacking hen house sure enough, and then no one will want to go there. So, stick to your guns, gentlemen."

One of her longtime ambitions was to attract more men to the food world. In France, where cooking had the status of a high art, men were the chief players whether or not they actually cooked: it was their talking, writing, and gourmandizing that put cuisine at the center of domestic and national life. In America, by contrast, cooking was traditionally defined as a female preoccupation, hence unworthy of serious attention. Julia had spent years in France trying to win the respect of male culinary authorities, self-appointed and otherwise, and had met with little success on account of her two handicaps: she was American and she was female. Yet the experience didn't turn her into a culinary feminist—quite the opposite. She was inclined to see men the way the French did: natural masters in the kitchen, born with an easy confidence at the stove, graced with an understanding of science and logic that guided them smoothly through the preparation of a meal. No matter that most American men couldn't cook. An aura of maleness in the world of American cookery would be enough to ennoble the whole enterprise, or so she hoped. When William Rice was appointed food editor of the *Washington Post* in 1972, she cheered. "I'm all for having MEN in these positions; it immediately lifts it out of the housewifery Dullsville category and into the important things of life!" Receiving fan letters from men gave her tremendous satisfaction, and she regularly assured her male correspondents that men made the best cooks.

Julia was adamant that her programs be aired in prime time, not only for the prestige but because having men in the audience made her work legitimate in her own eyes. Daytime television attracted only housewives—"And that's not our audience," she often said. Her audience, of course, was overwhelmingly female and packed with housewives, but when Julia said "housewife," she meant someone who didn't take food and cooking seriously. She knew very well there were countless women who weren't "housewives" in this sense; nonetheless, all "housewives" were women. If improvements were under way in American cooking and eating habits, it had to be men who deserved the credit. "Thank heaven for the men in our TV audience," she remarked in 1966. "They are responsible for stimulating interest in cooking. The women would just pass it over." When an interviewer asked her what she would say to young brides starting to cook, Julia's advice was to think about what men like to eat. "It will keep you away from those horrible gooky casseroles covered with canned mushroom soup and cornflakes," she went on. "Men don't like that stuff, and men are the people you want to feed." And, she added, be sure to buy solid, high-quality knives. "Just because the housewife doesn't know a great deal about equipment, she is often, unfortunately, taken in by glitter. If she went with her husband, he would not allow her to get a lot of this sort of flimsy junk, knives that are *pretty*." Women were too easily intimidated in the kitchen, Julia believed; they panicked if the recipe called for three tablespoons of lemon juice and they had only two. Men were fearless—in fact, men were accustomed to bullying, she once noted, which could be a very useful trait when faced with a recipe.

But while she was confident that men would have a good influence on the American home kitchen, their growing visibility in the culinary profession was a touchier subject. Yes, an infusion of talented male chefs was exactly what the profession needed in order to gain stature and respectability. But the ambitious young men taking up cooking included a number of homosexuals, and Julia feared they would soon define the profession, keeping straight men away. "It is like the ballet filled with homosexuals, so no one else wants to go into it." She urged a few close friends in the food world to encourage the "de-fagification" of cooking, but admitted that she had no idea how to go about it—and besides, "fags" bought plenty of cookbooks, including hers. "What to do!"

What she did, in the end, was generously support the career aspirations of every gifted cook who came her way—male or female, "normal" or not. Her devotion to "real male men" ran deep, but her appreciation for good cooking ran deeper still, and at this level she was entirely free of prejudice. Richard Olney, the moody American living on a Provençal hillside whose brilliant cooking impressed even the French, was a homosexual and not particularly friendly to Julia or most other people; she, in turn, never took to him personally. Yet she gave a press party when he published *Simple French Food* and used all her contacts to help him promote it, simply because his work was so outstanding. Another very skilled male cook of her acquaintance was "on the soft and wandlike side, feminine, but nicely so": this was a rare instance when she praised such traits in a man. And though she distanced herself from the women's movement in general, she spoke out readily against sex discrimination in the culinary profession. "You know, it wasn't until I began thinking about it that I realized my field is closed to women," she told a reporter in 1970. "It's very unfair. It's absolutely restricted. You can't get into the Culinary Institute of America in New Haven! The big hotels, the fancy New York restaurants, don't want women chefs." Her remark drew indignant letters from the director and the dean of women at the institute, pointing out that there were fully a dozen women among some 650 students. ("Julia and her sister Women's Lib advocates might also be pleased to hear that, if they don't get married first, each female has at least five good job offers by graduation.") By 1976, the institute had moved to Hyde Park, New York, and was doing so much better in regard to women that Julia agreed to speak at graduation. "Finally we have found out that women are people," she told the crowd. "It's a useful thing to know." In her own profession, she was a feminist in spite of herself: she simply would not put up with any injustice that threatened to deprive the world of a good chef. Julia funded scholarships for female culinary students, encouraged them to write to her about their progress, did a great deal of networking on behalf of young women chefs, and dispensed quantities of advice and encouragement. For her *Master Chefs* programs, she made a point of inviting male and female chefs in equal numbers; and she worked her media connections tirelessly to help cookbook writers she admired.

Julia's tangled sensibility about sex, gender, and food relaxed a good deal in the warmth of her friendship with James Beard, whom she loved and admired above anyone else in the American culinary world. Beard, a homosexual who neither hid nor flaunted his orientation, was widely recognized as the nation's leading authority on good cooking when Julia set out on her career. When she, Paul, and Simca went to New York for the launch of *Mastering*, Beard invited them to his house in Greenwich Village; and Julia very quickly recognized a soul mate. It was not an obvious match: Beard was self-taught, not professionally trained; his expertise was in American cookery, not French; and besides being homosexual, he was so extremely fat that he had none of the physical charms Julia normally liked in a man. But the two of them forged a bond that lasted until his death in 1985. They were both magnetic people, and when they turned that magnetism upon each other, they were captured simultaneously. Both were sharp, funny, and unpretentious; and both of them felt the same way about cooking—that it was endlessly and profoundly fascinating, that it deserved all the time and intelligence they could command, and that it was the greatest fun imaginable. A few months after they met, he was urging her to consider teaching at his school and touring with him so they could give joint lecture-demonstrations; she in turn wanted him to come to Boston and meet the people at WGBH—perhaps he could become involved in her new television series. "I would very much welcome the idea of doing something together," she told him. "I sense *une grande sympathie spirituelle*!" Beard was Julia's model for how to be a professional and how to be famous. She never forgot how generous he was when she arrived on the scene in 1961, a potential rival whom he greeted enthusiastically and introduced to everybody. "I think he has done much to set the tone of friendliness among cooking types, which is so different from that sniping and back-biting that goes on in France," Julia told M. F. K. Fisher. "Jim is such a hard worker, has such a vast store of knowlege in that enormous frame. There is outwardly some bluff in him, but I think that is because he is very tender inside." She used to say he was "cozy"—one of her favorite qualities in a man.

Julia rarely commented on Beard's homosexuality; she was far more concerned about the various health problems associated with his weight. Yet her homophobia came and went during their long friendship, apparently at random. "Good that people are out of the closet at last!" she noted in her journal in 1974, upon learning that an acquaintance was openly gay. "Makes things easier all around." A year later, she was agitating to keep "them" out of the culinary business. But by the 1980s, when the AIDS crisis began to unfold, the horror of what was happening to people she knew, and people she loved, dealt a significant blow to her longtime prejudice. "Last year my husband and I stood by helplessly while a dear and beloved friend went through months of slow and frightening agony," she told a crowd at Boston Garden in 1988 during an AIDS benefit sponsored by the American Institute of Wine and Food. "But what of those lonely ones? Those impoverished ones with no friends or family to ease the slow pain of dying? Those are the people we're concerned about this evening. And food is of very special importance here. Good food is also love." Her politics, her passions, and her fundamental decency were coming together at last. Some time after that, when a woman friend told her she was in love and about to marry another woman, Julia blanched for a second and then congratulated her warmly. What was important was the team.

Chapter 6

I Am Getting Very Tired of Kiwi Fruit

JULIA WAS SO enthusiastic about the idea of the National Beef Cook-Off, an annual cooking contest sponsored by the beef industry, that, in 1979, she agreed to be a judge and flew to Omaha. There were forty-nine beef dishes in competition, each a prizewinner at the state level, and the judges sat in a closed-off dining room tasting and discussing two dishes every half hour for two days. At 10:45 a.m. the first day, Julia finally tasted something she liked (Greek Beef Stew with Herb Biscuits), but the rest of the day proved disappointing. "Good idea—bad cook," she jotted on her scoring sheet after trying Pot 'n Cot Roast, and although she herself enjoyed Cantonese Beef Dinner, none of the other judges did. The next day started hopefully—Saucy Beef Taco Pizza was a success—but she let Mariachi Beefballs and Farmer Brown's Steak Supreme pass without comment. Best in show, she decided, was Fiesta Crepes en Casserole: cornmeal crepes stuffed with a mixture of beef, canned tomato sauce, canned creamed corn, and ready-made taco seasoning mix. A year later, Julia was back, enthusiasm undimmed, but after several rounds of tasting, she began to lose patience. "How to ruin a good piece of meat," she wrote next to Grilled Hawaiian Chuck Steak. Looking over the recipe for Spicy and Saucy Stuffed Round Steak, she scribbled, "What is 'beef sausage,' what is 'red cooking wine'?" One entry after another fell flat: "Tastes of the can." "Dead 'packaged' taste." "No real taste." First prize that year went to Baked Beef Brisket, made with only salt, pepper, garlic, onions, cornstarch, and water. "Tastes like food!" Julia noted gratefully.

She never returned to the Cook-Off, but she never gave up, either. Julia had a long, complicated relationship, much like a marriage, with American food. She was committed to it, and genuinely attracted, but the shortcomings, the character flaws, the willful misbehavior, and the sorry failures were constantly greeting her at the door. Thanks to a nature wonderfully capable of absorbing bad news with goodwill, her faith remained strong; but it was tested often. And if Mariachi Beefballs constituted one sort of betrayal, a bare slab of grilled fish surrounded by undercooked baby vegetables constituted another, perhaps worse. Sometimes it seemed to her that the food was becoming less and less appealing, even as Americans grew more sophisticated. "I am getting very tired of kiwi fruit and little juliennes of leeks," she said wearily in 1980. But she didn't tire of tuna fish sandwiches on rye. Or canned corned beef hash. Or hot dogs or chocolate ice cream sodas. And though she blanched at the sight of one of the Cook-Off entries—flapjacks folded over ground beef, garnished with strawberries, and doused with maple syrup—she dutifully tasted it. Then she brightened up, pronounced it delicious, and devoured the whole serving.

Julia had always been restless within the confines of traditional French cooking, especially during the years when she was becoming famous for it. To be sure, whenever she was working on a recipe with a recognized French name and heritage, she remained as faithful as possible to "*le vrai*" or "the real thing." Trying to re-create in Cambridge the Burgundian specialty of parslied ham in aspic, for instance, she found she had forgotten precisely how it should taste, and put the recipe aside until she could get back to France and restore her taste memory. But if she was simply pondering chicken, or dessert, or something good to eat, she relaxed. To her, French cooking wasn't a list of rules and ingredients, it was a set of techniques and a certain frame of mind. "I will never do anything but French cooking," she told *Time* in 1966, when she was being interviewed for the cover story. "It is much the most interesting and the most challenging and the best eating." She made this declaration, the magazine reported, "with Francophilic fervor." But a year or so earlier, for *The French Chef* she had invented a dessert she called *fantasie bourbonnaise*—peanuts, brown sugar, canned apricots, sliced bananas, and bourbon. "I just make up all the titles, as you can see," she told Simca cheerfully. By this time she was also employing instant mashed potatoes on occasion, stuffing crepes with whatever sounded appealing and setting them on fire ("People always seem to like this"), and rooting around for a decent paella recipe, testing French, Spanish, and American versions before settling on what she termed paella à la Julia. It all tasted good, and to her way of thinking, it was all French even if it wasn't "*kweezeene.*" She had been trained in France, her training shaped everything she did in the kitchen, and as long as she didn't pass off her inventions as time-honored recipes, she felt confident she was being true to what was important about French food. One day on *The French Chef,* she tossed spaghetti with chopped walnuts, olives, pimiento, and basil and called it spaghetti Marco Polo, urging viewers to eat it with chopsticks. Authentic? Sure, she argued: it was an authentically French way to think about dinner. "Taking ordinary everyday ingredients, and with a little bit of love and imagination, turning them into something appealing"—that was how the French cooked, she said, and that was how she cooked.

Nevertheless, every time the "Lasagne" and "Paella" programs were shown, or the "Curry Dinner" program, viewers were aghast. "You should be requested with all possible speed to confine yourself to the type of cooking you know well and leave the cuisines of other countries to those who know and respect it," wrote a typical distraught fan. Julia kept trying to explain—"It is the idea of lasagne, freed from ethnic restrictions and limitations," she wrote back—but this satisfied nobody. After 1972, when the last series of *French Chef* programs was taped, the word *French* disappeared from the titles of her books and television shows.

When it came to culinary technique, however, Julia was firm: this had to be French. Nothing else would do, because, as she often explained, French cuisine was the only one that had precise terminology and definite rules, an actual body of knowledge to be taught. Once you learned the rules, you could apply them to any other cuisine in the world. This parochial attitude toward cooking was very different from her wide-open attitude toward eating. Cooking appealed to her when she could imagine herself working within a clear intellectual structure, like a scientist of the sensual, mind and hands and palate fully engaged. A cuisine based on fresh ingredients handled minimally might produce wonderful meals, but it had no kitchen interest for her; and a cuisine that claimed its own complex technique—Chinese, for instance—she figured had to be French at heart. Julia had come to know and love Chinese food during her OSS years, and it remained her second-favorite cuisine, but as far as she was concerned, the best way to become a Chinese cook was to become a French cook first. "You would have already learned the basic ways to chop things up, and you'd just have to change your technique a bit to chop it up Chinese," she said blithely. As for Italian food, it could be very good to eat, but dropping pasta into boiling water was far too simple a procedure to result in what she called "food-type food." It was the French who had turned lasagna into something truly delicious. In fact, Julia remarked, whenever the French appropriated dishes from other countries, they always improved on the original. Like the chefs and Gourmettes who had been her guiding lights when she was learning to cook, Julia knew one true path and stuck to it. When aspiring chefs wrote her to ask where they should study, she always advised France, and she did her best to monitor French culinary schools so that her recommendations would be up-to-date. Here, in the realm of education, was the "Francophilic fervor" that *Time* had remarked upon. To learn cooking, to learn to dine with pleasure in a civilized manner, to learn the proper role of food in the life of a nation—France was the best classroom.

But it was very much a classroom and not a shrine. For all the rapture of her own introduction to France, and the pleasure she and Paul took in their beloved home in Provence, she had no patience with American food lovers who saw France through a fog of sentiment. The notion that French food, and French life, existed on some immeasurably blissful plateau unreachable by cloddish Americans was ridiculous to her. The whole point of learning the rules of French cooking was that they resulted in French food: there was nothing unreachable about the experience and no reason why home cooks couldn't re-create it in Pittsburgh.

The standard for lyrical evocations of culinary France had been set by M. F. K. Fisher, whose passionate following among food lovers and devotees of distinctive prose gave her the aura of a literary saint, especially after her first five books were republished as *The Art of Eating* in 1954. Julia admired Fisher's writing, and the two women were affectionate friends; but they had almost nothing in common except their fascination with food. Julia was a teacher: she liked clarity, facts, objectivity. Fisher was a writer from the school of impressionism: she liked artfulness, nuance, emotion. Their differences finally clashed in the mid-sixties, when Julia agreed to act as a "consultant and reader-over" on *The Cooking of Provincial France*, the first cookbook in a lavish new international series planned by Time-Life. M. F. K. Fisher had agreed to write the text. Her draft of the cookbook's introductory chapter was swept through with idyllic imagery: French housewives cooking by the seasons, markets full of delectable fresh produce, the family gathering daily for a multicourse midday dinner, old and young embraced by a glowing tradition that was forever France. Julia couldn't bear the rose-colored glasses. "She is seeing France from pre World War II eyes," she complained to Simca. Worse, in Julia's estimation, was the fact that France came off so splendidly in part because Fisher constantly compared it with America at its dreariest, as if nobody in the United States did anything at mealtimes but wolf down TV dinners. In her comments to Time-Life, Julia said Fisher was writing far too romantically. True, France was not yet enslaved to convenience, but changes were under way everywhere. "They are mechanizing in a French way, but those super markets, TV sets, dehydrated mashed potatoes and frozen fish are there to stay," she told the editors. At Julia's insistence, Fisher pulled back somewhat, but the final text was vivid with her conviction that French culinary tradition was rooted in French character and would never be fundamentally altered.

Julia didn't think there was much that was immutable about the French except their dogmatism; and though she loved the way they revered gastronomy, she refused to posit America as the opposite camp. She had spent far too many Paris evenings listening to Frenchmen dismiss all Americans as gastronomic idiots to sit through the same insults from Americans themselves. Like wave after wave of her American colleagues, Julia had arrived in France as an innocent, eaten the food in a state of wonder, and returned home with a calling. But unlike others who had experienced that life-changing moment, she never used her epiphany as a club to attack everything she had left behind. It simply wasn't in her to feel superior. "French cooking is not for the TV dinner and cake-mix set," she acknowledged as she was working on *Mastering*, so for the rest of her life she kept her attention fixed on everyone else—millions of her compatriots who, through no fault of their own, had never been taught to puree cauliflower with watercress or line a ramekin with caramel. The notion that French housewives were all wonderful cooks merely by virtue of being French—that they had acquired their skills by instinct and turned out fine meals, as Fisher put it in the Time-Life book, "as naturally as they breathe"—Julia found preposterous. "French women don't cook," she said firmly, many times. Living in Paris after the war, she had been one of the few middle-class wives she knew who did her own cooking, since servants were so widely available. Younger French homemakers had no such luxury—and as Julia pointed out, they were embracing frozen foods and other conveniences as happily as Americans had done years earlier. The difference was that America now had "hobby" cooks: men and women who cooked at home for the fun of it, and were becoming very good at traditional French dishes. "American families know their way around a kitchen far better than most French—and as our kitchens are so much easier to work in there is no limit to what we can do," she told a dubious Fisher. Julia liked to say that it would probably be Americans who kept alive the greatness of French cooking.

Even McDonald's, the chief target of the most vehement food critics, didn't strike Julia as all that bad. She and Paul had passed their first decade or so back in the United States largely ignoring the chain. As she told an interviewer in 1972, "We know where good food is located and we don't believe good food is to be found at McDonald's. So we don't go." But a year later, when *Time* asked for her opinion of the food, she went out for a meal and came back with a relatively benign review. "The buns are a little soft," she told *Time*. "The Big Mac I like least because it's all bread. But the French fries are surprisingly good. It's remarkable that you can get that much food for under a dollar. It's not what you would call a balanced meal; it's nothing but calories. But it would keep you alive." After that she spoke more and more positively about McDonald's, singling out the Quarter Pounder for special praise, though she made it clear she thought it was a big mistake to stop cooking the french fries in beef tallow. "They were so good!" she protested in a letter to the company. She did have one suggestion for improving the menu: in light of all those hamburgers being passed across the counter, McDonald's really should offer a decent red wine by the glass.

When it came to more ambitious restaurants, however, Julia put France firmly in the lead. She and Paul ate out very little during their first fifteen or twenty years in Cambridge, because the experience was so crushingly disappointing. They liked having lunch at the Ritz, in downtown Boston, and they welcomed Joyce Chen's, acclaimed as the first restaurant in the area to offer refined, authentic Chinese cooking. But for the most part, they ate at home, until a new generation of young American chefs—many inspired by Julia herself—began coming of age. The first local restaurant she was genuinely impressed by was the Harvest, on Brattle Street in Cambridge, where chef Lydia Shire started cooking in the mid-seventies. Julia was pleased to see a woman chef making good progress, and loved the food. But every time she and Paul returned to France, they were captivated all over again by the charm and professionalism of the restaurants, especially the informal bistros they liked best. They always had the traditional dishes they had ordered for years—"Simple things, like a soupe de poissons and a sole meunière"—and they basked in the atmosphere. "There is a seriousness of the cooking and serving, as well as an essential gaiety in the air that are like nothing else." At the three-star level, she thought French restaurants were much like their equivalents in New York; but the smaller places, to her, represented everything she loved about France.

French markets, on the other hand, couldn't begin to compare with what Julia fondly referred to as "my nice clean Star Market on Beacon St." When American food writers complained about pallid tomatoes and yellow plastic cheeses, or when chefs visiting from France told the press they couldn't buy what they needed in American markets because the quality was so poor, Julia was indignant. "Yesterday we did a quick shopping at San Peyre," she wrote to her family from Provence in 1977. "I thought to myself what a really disgusting market it was. The canned goods no one could complain of, but the meat was so revolting. Beef all dark red with limp yellow surrounding fat, no marbling, dried up edges. (The flies one is used to.) Everything looked simply disgusting. . . . Now that they can get everything from everywhere, we get just the same rock hard peaches, plums, pears and nectarines here as you get at home, that rot before they ripen." In the same letter she rejoiced in what was just coming into season—"We are finally getting local tomatoes, that yummy fresh garlic, and big white fresh onions, and those baby melons!" The moral was clear, and she preached it often: you have to shop carefully wherever you are.

That year, at home in Cambridge, she invited the innovative and widely admired French chef Michel Guérard to dinner and made lobster mayonnaise, saddle of lamb, broccoli, and a tarte tatin. It was a triumph of a meal, and as she told Simca proudly, "All this good food came from plain old markets." For the tart she had used Golden Delicious apples, which critics of the food system often singled out as representing the worst of American industrial farming: always available, always sturdy, always utterly bland. Guérard had praised everything, including the apples. "And I was interested that Guérard had no complaints about shopping, about butter, or cream, or vegetables, meat or fish," she added. She was particularly pleased that Guérard and his wife had raved about the broccoli, one of her favorite American vegetables and one unknown in France. He told her that he was going to plant some himself when he got home. Meanwhile, she fumed, writers such as Karen Hess and Waverly Root—two of the most prominent, and searing, critics of the food industry—were claiming that Americans ate nothing but slop. "What are these people talking about?" Julia demanded. "You can get disgusting things anywhere." If high-quality ingredients weren't available, she instructed, choose another recipe. Or buy the ingredients frozen or canned, and work them over until they tasted right.

The very idea that convenience products might have a

role in good cooking appalled purists, but Julia never rejected food just because it came from a factory. She thought bottled lemon juice was perfectly fine, and she liked the flavored salt sent to her by the manufacturer so much that she wrote back suggesting the company next put up a traditional *épices fines*, or French spice mixture, using the recipe from *Larousse Gastronomique.* "I always have to grind this up myself, but would love to have the exact copy in a bottle," she said—a statement so unabashedly American it would have made some of her colleagues in French cookery cringe. What mattered in most recipes was the cooking, Julia believed: a sloppy, mindless approach to the kitchen was far more damaging than any convenience product could possibly be. The reason she detested canned soup casseroles wasn't just that they tasted definitively of canned soup, but that they elevated speed over all other considerations. Real cooking took time. Real cooking took effort. Real cooking took a bit of intelligence. These particular ingredients were fundamental, and they were the very ones that tended to be missing from many American recipes, certainly those aimed at housewives. Once, as a favor to a longtime family friend, she agreed to look over the recipes in a church-affiliated cookbook and give her opinion on whether the book deserved wider distribution. Julia always tried to be honest when asked for an opinion; this time she was blunt as well. Any further distribution of this book would be a disservice to the entire country, she told her friend, and offered a few examples of what she meant.

> Page 75. Green beans with poppy seed dressing—canned green beans steeped in a mess of 1½ cups sugar, mustard, salt, onion juice, vinegar and salad oil. Ugh. "Farewell to the departing minister" is the title of this dinner, and one realizes why he left town. . . .
>
> Page 133. Packaged lime gelatin mixed with water, melted marshmallows, canned pineapple, cottage cheese, whipping cream and nuts. This is a ghastly horrible disgraceful kind of dish that no one should hear of, even less eat. And to push this kind of food onto the American public should be considered a felony.

It was probably the Jell-O that set her off—one of the few products that Julia held to be beyond redemption. But if she made common cause here with critics of American food and cooking, she broke with them on nearly every other issue. Julia didn't adopt any of her political positions automatically, any more than she would have praised a new cookbook without giving it careful study. By temperament and belief she was a liberal, but never a knee-jerk one. Gun control, censorship, abortion rights—on issues like these she was staunchly aligned with the left. But when food became a political issue, as it did during the 1970s, she carved out a position of her own that puzzled a good many of her colleagues and admirers. These were the years when journalists, food writers, and environmental activists began zeroing in on modern American agriculture and the food industry. In books, articles, and lawsuits they publicized the threat to human health and the damage to soil, water, and biodiversity posed by chemical-heavy factory farming; and they vociferously mourned the loss of taste and texture in fruits, vegetables, and meats. Other aspects of the American way of culinary life—convenience products, overpackaging, artificial ingredients, the supermarket system itself—tumbled into disrepute as well. Gastronomes had never admired the technological sheen of the American food supply, and now it was a full-fledged object of scorn.

Julia had little sympathy with this movement, in part because she refused to think of the food industry as an enemy. Since the earliest years of her career, whenever she wanted reliable information on anything from flour to seafood, she habitually wrote to the major food companies or to such trade organizations as the Dairy Council, the Meat and Livestock Board, and the Egg Board. "I don't know as much as I would like to know about rice, and would very much appreciate any documentation you might be so kind as to give," she once wrote to the Rice Council, adding that she wanted "deeply technical documentation (*not* typical housewife stuff which doesn't go deeply enough into things)." Such queries brought a steady supply of industry-generated literature to her mailbox (including, in this case, "Reduction of Cohesion in Canned Pearl Rice by Use of Edible Oil Emulsions and Surfactants"), which she pored over eagerly. When it came to a standoff between these long-trusted sources and the activists who were assailing them, she sided with her sources. Pesticides?

Hormones in beef cattle? Antibiotics in chickens? She researched these problems by going to the same sorts of experts she had always trusted in the past, and took their word as objective.

Her distrust of health-minded reformers in the food world also went back many years. She had been battling nutritionists ever since she described in *Mastering*, and then demonstrated on television, the proper French way to cook green vegetables—namely, in a large quantity of rapidly boiling water. Nutritionists and home economists wrote to complain that all the vitamins went down the drain, and that the approved method was to cook vegetables in as little water as possible. Julia always countered that the vegetables were so much tastier when prepared by her method that people ate more, and thus took in many more vitamins. But the criticism irritated her: she called the early health-food advocate Adele Davis "that dreadful woman" and said that Davis's vegetables were so limp and gray, no wonder she had to take vitamin pills. The very idea that people could look upon food as medicine, that they might sit down to eat thinking only about their arteries or their risk of cancer, appalled Julia; and she fought it long and hard. "The dinner table is becoming a trap rather than a pleasure," she often said, and she once pointed out that she'd never met a "healthy, normal nutritionist who loves to eat." When articles about cholesterol began appearing in the sixties, she made a firm decision not to believe them. Even after she finally conceded the importance of cutting down on fat, and began devising lighter recipes, she retained a sacred place for butter and cream in her cooking. "In this book, I am very conscious of calories and fat," she assured readers in *The Way to Cook,* her magnum opus published in 1989. Sure enough she included "low-fat cookery" in the index and listed some two dozen recipes under that heading. Every time she offered a dish such as Broiled Fish Steaks au Natural, however, she suggested a few good ways to perk it up: namely, Lemon-Butter Sauce, Winey Cream Sauce, a hollandaise, a béarnaise, or at the very least "1½ to 2 Tbs soft butter, optional."

As for organic food, as far as Julia was concerned it was even worse than health food. In 1971, she received a newsletter from the United Fresh Fruit and Vegetable Association, a trade group, which featured an essay titled "The 'Organic Food' Kick," by R. A. Seelig. Julia read it, photocopied it, often quoted it, and used it as the basis of much of her thinking about food reformers. "In the real world of farming today there is no room for the cult that regards 'natural methods' as good, and all improvements on nature as bad," Seelig wrote. "Many of the organic food cultists, who go arm in arm with the 'health food' faddists, appear to have a semi-religious conviction that what is natural is a manifestation of God's purpose, while what is scientific is a denial of God's plan." This was the sort of language guaranteed to set Julia squarely against advocates of organic farming. She and Paul avoided all manifestations of organized religion; and the lesson Julia had drawn from her own conversion experience, back at the Cordon Bleu, was that science and logic easily trumped instinct and faith at every stage of cooking. "I just do not want to be allied to any cultist type of operation, which this could well turn out to be," she told a group called CHEFS (Chefs Helping to Enhance Food Safety), which was enlisting chefs to promote organic farming. "I am for hard scientific facts."

The scientific facts that most appealed to her were those offered up by such organizations as the American Council on Science and Health, a group funded in part by the food industry and notorious among reformers for taking the industry's point of view on everything from sugar-laden breakfast cereals to genetically modified tomatoes. Julia became a financial supporter of the council and appeared at one of its press events. She called the genetic engineering of food "one of the greatest discoveries" of the twentieth century, spoke out in favor of irradiation as a food safety measure while terming opponents "Nervous Nellies," and agreed to provide a testimonial in favor of monosodium glutamate when it came under attack in 1991. Since she had always disliked MSG, she rejected the wording offered by the industry ("Like all chefs, I have used MSG as an ingredient in recipes for years") and instead called MSG "a harmless food additive that can make good food taste even better." What was truly "evil," she added, was to frighten the public with misinformation.

The one area of food safety in which she readily sided with the reform organizations was the problem of contamination in shellfish. When a subcommittee of the House of Representatives held hearings on the subject, Julia agreed to supply written testimony, and she discussed the issue in public on other occasions as well. "Only a small percentage of the fish and shellfish sold in this country is inspected for wholesomeness by government agents," she told a meeting of the Newspaper Food Editors and Writers Association in 1988. The solution was supposed to be thorough cooking, "but who wants to cook an oyster till it's a piece of cement?" Fish cookery was dear to her heart, and anything that interfered with a lovely poached oyster garnish for sole *à la Normande* in her estimation plainly deserved a major public outcry.

For the most part, however, Julia was unable to make the connection between enjoying food and working to radically overhaul the food system. To forge precisely such a connection was the aim of the second wave of culinary enthusiasts, the ones inspired by Alice Waters, whose Chez Panisse restaurant opened in Berkeley in 1971 and spawned the revolution known as California cuisine. Though Waters and her colleagues shared some of the philosophy behind nouvelle cuisine, the much-hyped effort on the part of French chefs to invigorate classic cooking by making it lighter, less formulaic, and more sharply focused on fresh ingredients, the spirit of the California movement was very different. The burden of the past wasn't an issue for American restaurants. Waters had been dazzled by the clarity and depth, the almost voluptuous simplicity of the home cooking she tasted in the French countryside. She opened Chez Panisse with a dream of re-creating that food in Berkeley—which meant her chefs had to start, as those countryside cooks started, with the ingredients around them. This emphasis on ingredients was what made America's newest cuisine a political movement as well as a gastronomic one. Its aim was to reduce the reach of agribusiness while promoting the incomparable flavors of ingredients that came directly from nearby growers—to put a fresh, local chicken in every pot.

Waters lavished attention and support upon the small farms, ranches, bakeries, and dairies that could supply her with jewellike products; and her chefs applied their considerable skills to showcasing the bounty that arrived in the kitchen each day. Chez Panisse was enormously influential, and chefs across the country began doing their own versions of what was happening in Berkeley, eventually calling it New American cooking. As often as not the watchwords associated with Chez Panisse—"local," "seasonal," "organic"—were honored only sporadically in the restaurants that came later. Nonetheless, a powerful new perspective on sophisticated cooking, one that gave pride of place to the freshness and quality of the raw materials, settled in among chefs, food writers, and adventurous home cooks.

Julia saw most of the elaborate innovations wrought in the name of nouvelle cuisine as an appalling insult to the logic and dignity of fine French cooking, and California cuisine struck her as an equally bad idea. She didn't like the food, and she didn't like the high-minded, purist approach to shopping and cooking. Great cooking meant, as she often said, doing something to the food, not serving a few slices of humanely raised veal on a plate with three perfect radishes and calling it dinner. She didn't even like humanely raised veal; she thought it was tasteless. This worshipful approach to ingredients, she told a San Francisco magazine, "takes us away from cuisine as an art form into something that I believe is much too simple, too tiresome." Worse, the emphasis on organic, artisanal ingredients put California cuisine far beyond the reach of most Americans, who shopped in supermarkets and had never seen a pea shoot or a leaf of baby arugula in their lives. Julia's entire career was predicated on supermarkets, and she couldn't see the point of promoting a cuisine that was too rarefied to be supplied by Safeway or Stop & Shop.

Many of Julia's devoted followers could hardly believe what they were hearing when she voiced some of her most pro-industry opinions. "*You*, of all my favorite people!" exclaimed a fan who had discovered that Julia saw nothing wrong with irradiating the food supply. But in Julia's view, her positions weren't pro-industry, they were pro-food. Unless there was incontrovertible evidence of danger, she was wholly opposed to any measure that restricted food choices, or ruled out a particular category of food, or put any kind of food in a bad light. As she saw it, irradiation didn't pose nearly the threat that, say, vegetarianism did. To find cruelty in every steak and cholesterol in every spoonful of cream, to sneer at the string beans because they came from a box in the freezer—this wall of suspicion between Americans and their meals was far worse than anything in the food itself. "If fear of food continues, it will be the death of gastronomy in the United States," she told an interviewer in 1990. Julia could taste the difference between a free-range chicken and its factory counterpart, but she refused to believe good cooking called for a degree of wariness normally associated with managing a chronic disease.

Soon after she began on television in 1963, the venerable Boston company S. S. Pierce, which sold an extensive line of canned fruits, vegetables, and meats, asked her to write an article about cooking with such pantry items, to be published in the company catalog. Julia was pleased with the assignment—it would be another year before she made her decision to turn down all commercial offers—and set about testing dozens of S. S. Pierce products. Tiny Whole Carrots she found very good, especially when she cooked them in her own brown glazing sauce with parsley, but Chicken à la King needed quite a bit of help from chopped sautéed ham, scallions, hard-boiled eggs, tarragon, a bit of cornstarch for thickening, and some vermouth. No matter what she did to the cream of avocado soup, it was poor, and the canned chicken was undeniably stringy, though marinating it in a vinaigrette and adding homemade mayonnaise made it tastier.

If there was anything ironic about how hard she had to

work in order to make these so-called convenience foods acceptable, Julia didn't see it. To her, they were just fruits, vegetables, and meats; and like any other ingredients, they needed the best a cook could give them. Picking up a can of S. S. Pierce tuna, she decided to write a recipe for the most famously convenient, famously derided supper dish in the American repertoire—and to make a version worthy of any dinner table she knew, including her own.

> Place about 2 cups of drained canned tuna in a bowl. Flake the fish, then fold in two thirds of your cream sauce. Fold in also, if you wish, 2 or 3 sliced hard-boiled eggs and ⅓ cup of coarsely grated Swiss cheese. Correct seasoning. Spread seasoned and buttered cooked rice or noodles in the bottom of a 2½-quart casserole, turn the sauced fish over it, and cover with the remaining sauce. Sprinkle with 2 or 3 tablespoons of grated Swiss cheese and a tablespoon of butter cut into dots. Half an hour before you are ready to serve, set the casserole in a preheated 375-degree oven until bubbling hot and the top has browned. This makes a delicious main course, and needs only a green salad and a nice white Bordeaux or rosé wine to make quite a feast.

Surely this was the only tuna casserole recipe ever devised that included the instruction "Correct seasoning."

Chapter 7

She Likes to Eat

JULIA NEVER USED the word *gourmet.* She did have a soft spot for *gourmette,* at least when it was associated with her favorite organization of food-minded women in Paris; but *gourmet* as most Americans paraded around the term conjured to Julia an odious mix of pretension, snobbery, and ignorance. When she and Simca and Louisette were trying to think up a name for their school, they decided to call themselves "gourmandes" instead. A gourmand, Julia explained, was "one who knows good food thoroughly and has a fine appetite." Later, working on the introduction to *Mastering,* she experimented with the phrasing of a theme she would return to again and again, whenever anyone asked who her audience was, or precisely which Americans were out there roasting squabs and setting them atop liver canapés. "We've visualized our readers simply as those who love to eat and love to cook & want a working knowledge of French techniques," she wrote in the draft. Here and forever, the operative word was *love.* In other notes for the introduction, she called the book "serious & loving," and she said it was aimed at "people who love to eat, for they are the great cooks of this world." Or, as she put it to Avis early in their friendship, "People who love to eat are always the best people." Eagerness, appetite, a willingness to work, and the constant delight of discovery—for Julia, loving food and loving life were the same. "Why is French cooking so good?" she asked herself once, composing the beginning of a magazine article as she sat surrounded by the notes, recipes, and reference books that abundantly fed her workdays. "It is love that makes it so."

Julia loved food in many ways, and for many reasons. Deliciousness was always a good reason to love something she had just tasted, but awfulness had charms as well. The first time she encountered English food in all its legendary misery, she was entranced: "There, on an immense white platter, sprawling over a mound of wet rice, lay several large, bony, yellowish pieces of thoroughly boiled fowl, each portion partially masked by a thickish white paste through which protruded chicken hairs, slowly waving." Every moment of that bleak meal lived up to its reputation, and she cherished the experience. On another occasion, at their house in Provence, she dipped a madeleine into a *tisane*, or French herbal tea, and nearly swooned with delight. It wasn't that she loved the taste—the madeleine was a mediocre one from a shop—but that she loved tasting exactly what Proust was talking about. The combination really did produce a unique flavor, one that might well linger beyond memory until released by the dip of another madeleine decades later. "She couldn't get over it," Avis told friends afterward.

Food was a restorative, too, the only one she knew. Julia's preferred treatment for her rare colds was to climb into bed with a bourbon on ice; but if emotions were at issue, she turned immediately to the kitchen. Working with food was more than a source of comfort, it was how she prodded herself to keep moving forward. In 1968, she discovered a lump in her breast, and when she woke up in the hospital after the biopsy, she found she had been given a radical mastectomy. The doctor had warned her of the possibility, but it was still a shock. At first she just sat in the bathtub and cried. "The first view of that mutilated side is far from pleasant," she recalled later. But as soon as she could, she went straight to work on tripe. What better way to recuperate? As long as she was stuck at home, she might as well figure out how to get squeamish Americans to eat the lining of a cow's stomach. The very thought of those delectable morsels simmering away for twelve hours with carrots, leeks, garlic, wine, and a few pig's feet lifted her spirits.

Whatever she was cooking, the chief ingredient was her joyful fanaticism. She relished every opportunity to eviscerate and cut up a whole chicken or a fish—"I time myself every time just to see how fast," she told Avis—and Paul often described hearing "my tender little wifelet" crash around the kitchen whacking and chopping with enthusiasm, occasionally chastising the cat in French. She gloried in a meal of foie gras marinated in Madeira and cognac, stuck with truffles, wrapped in a pig's caul, and poached—"We all ate it with a spoon, 8 of us, and we ate every bit of it"—and she just as happily anticipated the long span of lunches following Christmas because she would get to have her favorite leftovers every single day (cold turkey, Virginia ham, homemade mayonnaise, and cherry tomatoes). Eggplant, she once mused to her editor Judith Jones, should always be purchased young, firm, and unwrinkled, like "the lovely nubile elbows, arms and knees of Radcliffe freshmen." Years after completing the exhaustive recipe research for both volumes of *Mastering*, she could still throw herself into a culinary challenge as rapturously as a dog chasing a Frisbee. To spend days ferreting out the best way to prepare the lemons for a lemon tart exhilarated her; after a marathon of twenty-five strawberry soufflés, she couldn't wait to try one more that she thought would be better. Even late in her career, she made a point of developing new recipes every time she gave a class or demonstration. Her audiences wouldn't have minded if she did a recipe she had already published, but Julia wanted to keep challenging herself, keep pushing forward on what she called "the life work." There were only two things she hated doing in the kitchen: deep-fat frying, because of the mess and the smell, and making hors d'oeuvres, which were just too dainty for her liking. Julia's idea of cocktail party food was a good, thick ham sandwich.

Once a writer for *Cosmopolitan* asked her to name her

favorite "binge" foods. Julia said she didn't have any: "Maybe life itself is the proper binge," she remarked. When she said this, in 1975, she was nearly a year into the most stressful period of her life: Paul's long slow deterioration following heart surgery and a series of strokes. For some fifteen years he gradually lost stamina and mental functioning, as well as much of his personality. It was the end of the team as a working enterprise, but Julia honored what remained as long as she possibly could. Wherever she went—to a television rehearsal or taping, a business meeting, a reception in her honor, a dinner party—Paul accompanied her just as he always had. On a trip to Washington in 1976, he participated in all the publicity events including radio programs. "Even if he answered quite other things than the questions posed, it made little difference," Julia reported. "So we shall just go on as usual, as long as he is happy." He still looked over the mail and jotted comments on it, but his once-graceful handwriting was shaky, and his notes in the margins were plaintive: "I find this impossible to understand." "What is this about!" Sometimes he dozed off at the dinner table or became confused or angry because he couldn't follow the conversation; often the two of them left social events early. Julia never made apologies for her silent, sometimes difficult companion, though she used to poke him when he dropped off at dinner. "He is generally happy and says people just don't think or talk clearly and no wonder nobody understands what's going on!" she told Simca in 1985. "As long as he feels that way, we're saved."

Two years later his condition had worsened so markedly that Julia was forced to admit he was "truly on the downhill grade," but even then she was incapable of dwelling on the dark side. "Fortunately he does not know the state he is in, and remains in good humor with, so far, good enough appetite," she told Simca. "And thank heaven I have plenty of work to do." France dropped away from their life during these years, and they traded in the long Cambridge winters for Santa Barbara, where Julia bought an apartment by the sea. Finally, in 1989, she was forced to put him in a nursing home, where she visited several times a day and called between visits. He died five years later.

Julia cried readily, when life warranted it, but she never felt sorry for herself. Her own death was an event she rarely contemplated—"May we all go out like rockets, rather than delayed fuses!"—though she thought it was sensible to plan for old age. Long before she needed it, she made sure she had a place reserved at a retirement complex in Santa Barbara for what she called "the final days." She knew she would outlive Paul, and she had no intention of being "old Mrs. Non-compos in a big Cantabridgian mansion." As Paul faded from her, however, she found she was increasingly aware of what it meant to grow old without children. She had never poured a great deal of regret into the fact that she couldn't have children; she simply accepted it. But now, as she told Simca, she could see the difference between childless women like themselves, and someone like Avis, who had children and grandchildren around her in her last years. "Eh bien, we shall take care of ourselves," was the characteristic way Julia wound up this train of thought. As it turned out, her last years overflowed with family, friends, and colleagues, including—to her delight—a tall, engaging widower named John McJannet, with whom she kept company for several years in the 1990s.

Reporters frequently asked what she would eat if she were sitting down to her last meal. Oysters, she often said, and roast duck. A delicious salad, a perfectly ripe pear, a taste of chocolate. Once an interviewer wanted to know what she would prepare if she were cooking a meal for God. Julia was a devout atheist, but not where food was concerned. She was happy to contemplate a meal so exquisite the creator of the world would be very glad he had gone to all the trouble. "To show him the wonders of the earth?" she asked. "Well, we did a lovely dish of poached fresh artichoke bottoms filled with oysters in a white butter sauce and that was awfully nice. You could add some truffles, too. Then, I would make one of my duck recipes, some lovely fresh asparagus, and some braised Belgian endive, and some of my fresh French rolls." A puff pastry dessert with raspberries, and then a little sherbet completed this offering, which to Julia constituted a fine definition of the sacred.

But on one occasion, when it was the food lover and

restaurateur George Lang who asked her the last-meal question for a magazine column, she wrote out a response in such thoughtful detail that she really did seem to be imagining life's farewell banquet. She began with the most important element of all: "My last meal would be cooked at home with a friend or two that I like to cook with." There would be six at table, always the number she considered just right for a dinner party, and they would start with Cotuit oysters, "accompanied by very thinly sliced homemade rye bread, lightly buttered." Caviar and vodka next, then "some very fresh, fine, green California asparagus," and for the main course one of her favorite duck dishes—"the one in which you roast the duck until the breast is rare and then cook the legs and wings separately en confit, with a very nice light port wine sauce." Peas and *pommes Anna* would be served, and a great wine, "probably a light Burgundy or a St.-Émilion." The salad would be just lettuce and endive, with lemon and French olive oil in the dressing, and she might give it a sprinkling of walnuts. "I like salad and cheese together, but we would also have wine because the salad would have practically no acid in it," she explained. A Burgundy might be just right, depending on the cheeses, and she specified not only the bread but the bakery—"really good French bread, probably from Les Belles Miches and some of the Santa Barbara sour dough." For dessert, her own beloved charlotte Malakoff and a Château d'Yquem. Ripe grapes and a Comice pear, perhaps chocolate truffles with coffee, and "a fine selection of great liqueurs"—calvados, framboise, prune, and marc de Bourgogne—would round out the dinner. "At least that meal would suit me now," she reflected, "and probably would then, at the very end, before we all slipped off the raft."

The meal that suited her at the very end was quite a bit simpler. In 2004, Julia was living in Santa Barbara, increasingly frail after a year marked by knee surgery, a bout of postoperative complications and infections, kidney failure, more knee surgery, and a stroke. Recuperating from the knee surgery had been agonizing: it was so painful to stand up, and she was still so weak from the stroke that for the first time in her life she refused to try. Her longtime assistant, Stephanie Hersh, told the rehabilitation staff to move Julia's wheelchair to a kitchen and ask her to chop some onions. It worked—the kitchen counter itself seem to draw her to her feet, and rehab could begin. But over the next months, her world shrank and her days became meager. She had liked going for drives and to the movies, but these became impossible; she could no longer sit at the computer and work; she slept a great deal. Friends came by for short visits, which she enjoyed; and food was a source of delight to the end. Stephanie knew Julia's appetite very well after so many years together, and on August 11, she made a pot of onion soup, using the recipe from *Mastering*. The aroma of a rich onion soup was always one of Julia's favorites—"That's a wonderful smell and a very appetizing one," she had declared on *The French Chef*, breathing in the heady fragrance of onions, butter, bouillon, and wine. She had the soup for dinner that August night, and ate with pleasure. The next day, her doctor called to report that Julia had picked up an infection and had to be hospitalized for treatment. Julia was reluctant. Would it make her better? she asked. No, he said, not really. She decided against treatment. It was time to leave: she had had all she wanted, she was grateful, and she was full. Stephanie settled her into bed for a nap, with the cat on the covers next to her, and Julia never woke up. She died early in the morning of August 13, two days before her ninety-second birthday.

In the months following Julia's death, many people took down their old copies of *Mastering* and made farewell dinners; others offered their best imitations of her inimitable voice; and just about everyone who remembered her on television lifted a glass to send a heartfelt "*Bon appétit!*" in the general direction of paradise. Her fans, who had long ago stopped making veal Prince Orloff, if indeed they ever attempted it, never forgot what they absorbed from Julia about good cooking. Learn how to do this, she would say, picking up a knife or an egg or a wriggling lobster. Try this, you can do it. Determination was what mattered, skill was the only shortcut they would ever need, and anything taking a long time was probably worth it. The food industry was spending millions to hammer home precisely the opposite message, but Julia had a source of power greater even than a national ad budget could purchase: people trusted her. She was the rare celebrity who never fell from grace.

In the obituaries and remembrances that followed her death, she was often hailed as the person who led us out of the canned soup fifties into a land flowing with boutique wines and fusion cuisine—or, as her achievement was often summed up, the woman who introduced us to quiche. Nobody knew better than Julia that she had not, in fact, introduced us to quiche. As early as 1957, when she was living in Washington, she wrote to Simca to let her know that recipes for quiche lorraine and coquilles St. Jacques were circulating widely and had become "very well known here"—not like pizza, to be sure, but hardly novelties. Sophisticated home cooking had a decent constituency in the land of the cake mix long before *Mastering* appeared. What Julia did do first, and single-handedly, was to make sophisticated home cooking count. She made it impossible to ignore. Publishers, food editors, television executives, the food industry—everyone who believed that American women were pledged for all eternity to frozen chicken potpies had to rethink a great many assumptions in the wake of *The French Chef.* Cookbooks themselves changed, as publishers saw an eager readership developing for books that explained technique as well as offering recipes. True, most people in the 1960s and 1970s would no sooner have opened one of Julia's books in search of dinner than they would have climbed on a unicycle to get to work. Family meals across the nation still centered on long-familiar recipes for meat loaf and pork chops; and dieting had established its own ceaseless track through the kitchen. But

Julia's startling leap to fame with cassoulet and white-wine fish sauces could not be dismissed. Apparently, some people really did want to buy whisks and shallots and food processors, and really did want to try lengthy recipes for French, or Chinese, or Italian, or Indian food. If that was the case, nobody in the culinary business was going to stand in the way. The success of her books and television programs created a permanent and ever-expanding niche market for good food in America.

The legacy Julia herself had in mind was not confined to the kitchen. In the last fifteen or twenty years of her life, she thought a great deal about what it would take to establish gastronomy as an academic discipline—"like architecture," she told a reporter in 1989. "It took architects years to get established, to show that it was not just a purely artisanal affair, and that's what I hope will happen. It would be a fine arts degree just like any other, but majoring in gastronomy." Much of her time and energy, and an immense amount of her celebrity, were put to the service of this dream. She lobbied hard for Boston University to set up such a program, and was rewarded in 1991 when BU began offering a master of liberal arts degree in gastronomy through its Metropolitan College. In 1996, New York University established a program in food studies at both the undergraduate and graduate levels; and as the idea caught on around the country, food studies came to be recognized as one of the liveliest and fastest-growing disciplines in academia. Julia was also a vigorous supporter of the Schlesinger

Library at Harvard, which houses one of the nation's most substantial culinary collections. She donated her own papers and persuaded Simca and Avis to do the same, and her participation in library events brought it considerable visibility. She liked to think that someday all the culinary collections in the United States would be "connected by computer," with the Schlesinger at the center of a national research network buzzing constantly with new findings and ideas. "Me, I am not an intellectual," she had said ruefully to Avis years earlier. But of course she was—her passion for food raced through her whole body and fired her brain as well. One of her lasting gifts to the food world was to help make it a place where good minds could settle in for life.

French cooking, Julia style, flourished at countless dinner parties for a decade or so, but eventually gave way to simpler, lighter cuisines. Though *Mastering* remains the gold standard for learning French techniques and recipes, it's a rare host or hostess who makes an entire, head-spinning meal from Julia's repertoire the way her early fans sometimes did. By the time she died, American cooking reflected far more direct influences from California and Italy than from any of Julia's books, and the culinary stage she had once dominated was crowded with stars. Julia welcomed all of them; she was always looking for what she called "new blood" for the profession. Yet it's doubtful whether any of the prolific, telegenic cooking experts who came after Julia have ever touched an audience the way she did. Today there appear to be two kinds of good cooks: those who want to impress people and those who want to feed people. The meal may be delicious in either case, but you can always tell the difference, in part because it's written across the face of the cook when he or she presents the platter. "Admire me," some of their expressions seem to say. "Here, this is for you, let's eat!" say the others. Julia's ego was never visible when she cooked: it seemed to flow directly into the food and emerge as a gift of herself. "Thank you!" people often wrote in their fan letters. It was the first thing they wanted to tell her. They understood—watching her ecstatically smell a vanilla bean, or nail an eel by the head to a board for easier peeling, or put a freshly baked baguette to her ear ("Now this *crackles*!"), or hold up a spoon with its miraculous cloud of beaten egg whites—that she was teaching them how to live.

SOURCES

JULIA CHILD gave nearly all her personal and professional papers to the Schlesinger Library at Harvard; and in those dozens of cartons I found most of the material for the facts, inferences, and quotations in this book. The library also holds the papers of Avis DeVoto, whose correspondence provided details on the publishing of *Mastering the Art of French Cooking* as well as other insights into Julia's life and times.

Among secondary sources, the most important to me was Noel Riley Fitch's *Appetite for Life: The Biography of Julia Child* (Doubleday, 1997), which I drew on especially in describing Julia's childhood in California, her education, and her life just after college. *Sisterhood of Spies: The Women of the OSS*, by Elizabeth P. McIntosh (Naval Institute Press, 1998), supplied information on Julia's wartime experiences. Hundreds of journalists interviewed Julia over the years, but the most substantive articles remain the *Time* cover story (November 25, 1966) and the profile by Calvin Tomkins in *The New Yorker* (December 23, 1974). I made use of both, and occasionally of other newspaper and magazine stories as well.

To describe and quote from Julia's television programs, I used notes and transcripts in the Schlesinger archives, and the DVDs of *The French Chef* produced by WGBH Boston Video.

I'm sorry that the Penguin Lives format does not include footnotes, but researchers who would like to track down specific references are invited to write to me care of the publisher.

ACKNOWLEDGMENTS

I AM INDEBTED first and forever to Fern Berman, who called me one day with a really good idea for a book. In the course of the research that followed, I received generous help from Marilyn Mellowes, Stephanie Hersh, Joan Reardon, Clark Wolf, Patty Unterman, Linda McJannet, Rebecca Alssid, Fran Carpentier, Judith Jones, and Ken Schneider, and librarians at the Boston Public Library and the Smithsonian Institution. As always, the staff at the Schlesinger Library supported my research with assistance that was not only efficient but constantly enlightening.

PERMISSIONS

Grateful acknowledgment is made to the following for permission to publish excerpts from letters and other writings:

Julia Child Foundation for Gastronomy and the Culinary Arts, William A. Truslow, Trustee.

Arthur and Elizabeth Schlesinger Library on the History of Women in America, Radcliffe Institute for Advanced Study, Harvard University.

Mark DeVoto for the Avis DeVoto letters in the Schlesinger Library, Harvard University.

Penguin
LIVES